Parenting

the

Prodigal

Parenting
the
Prodigal

S. Rutherford McDill Jr.

HERALD PRESS
Scottdale, Pennsylvania
Waterloo, Ontario

Library of Congress Cataloging-in-Publication Data
McDill, S. R. (S. Rutherford)
    Parenting the prodigal / S. Rutherford McDill, Jr.
      p. cm. — (University seminars/Leonard Hastings Schoff
memorial lectures)
    Includes bibliographical references and index.
    ISBN 0-8361-9042-4 (alk. paper)
    1. Parent and teenager. 2. Problem youth. 3. Parenting.
4. Parenting—Religious aspects—Christianity. I. Title.
II. Series.
HQ799.15.M375 1996
649'.153—dc20   96-22680
                                            CIP

All Bible quotations are used by permission, all rights reserved and are from *The Holy Bible, New International Version*, copyright © 1973, 1978, 1984 International Bible Society, Zondervan Bible Publishers.

PARENTING THE PRODIGAL
Copyright © 1996 by Herald Press, Scottdale, Pa. 15683
    Published simultaneously in Canada by Herald Press,
    Waterloo, Ont. N2L 6H7. All rights reserved
Library of Congress Catalog Number: 96-22680
International Standard Book Number: 0-8361-9042-4
Printed in the United States of America
Book and cover design by Paula M. Johnson
Cover photo by Jim Whitmer

05 04 03 02 01 00 99 98 97 96 9 8 7 6 5 4 3 2 1

Dedication

No one can know the suffering that parents of prodigals go through night after night, worrying, hoping, praying, crying, dying a little every time their phone rings late at night. No one can know the sadness and emptiness parents feel when they look at the spaces their child used to fill up with play and joy and laughter. No one can know the confusion, guilt, despair parents feel when they retrace their child's journey into prodigality and wonder what they could have done to cause it or did not do but should have.

No one can know—except parents who have been there.

This book is dedicated to those parents.

Contents

Acknowledgments

THERE ARE SCORES of unsung heroes behind every book, and their incalculable value in the process of finishing cannot be overestimated or overstated. I extend my heartfelt thanks to—

Dr. R. Robert King for his encouraging comments and helpful suggestions toward filling in the gaps the author thought were already filled. As any writer knows, what is in the brain does not always flow onto paper in its completed form. Sometimes writers need other critical thinkers/readers to follow along behind, prodding them to fill in the spaces left gaping open. Dr. King played this role.

Herald Press and its team of editors, S. David Garber in particular.

Carol Lacy, a special friend and co-laborer in writing, who nurtured this project from start to finish as agent, critic, encourager, wordsmith, consultant, adviser, and most importantly, as translator. She took pedagogical narrative and made it palatable.

Author's Preface

THE PAGES THAT FOLLOW have been a long time coming. The idea underlying this project was germinated by a brief scene in one of Focus on the Family's first video series. During a seminar intermission a group of audience members gathered around Dr. James Dobson (head of Focus on the Family) asking questions. With cameras still rolling, one worried lady asked Jim a question pertaining to what could be done with a child who had become extreme in his defiance.

Jim's response was not encouraging. He somberly admitted that rebellious children can get so far out of parental control that they essentially have parents over a barrel, with little left for parents to do about it except damage control, and not much of that.

As a young practicing family therapist and psychologist, and a father, Dobson's words hit me like a bomb. Surely there were things a parent could do if his imagination were fertile enough to devise new and unorthodox ways of dealing with juvenile misbehavior. Surely an adult, full of experience and the emotional wherewithal to outlast and outmaneuver an adolescent, could turn things around. The saying, "Old age and treachery can always overcome youth and enthusiasm" seemed to apply here. Why not use some of the craftiness and cunning picked up in life to the advantage of parents and prodigals?

Far too many parents have tried shoving matches to move their prodigals around, only to learn that shoving won't and can't work. With each step the prodigal takes away from parental influence and control, it seems parents ratchet up their level of pushiness until the prodigal indeed back-steps out of parental reach, and parents collapse in an exhausted heap, ruing the day their child was born.

This book condenses the lessons learned from countless families who have come through my practice. It had to wait until I had completed my own parenting and had launched my own children into adulthood. Now I can reflect on what worked and what didn't, not only in my own parenting, but in the parenting lives of the families with whom I have had the undeserved privilege of working over two decades of practice before my retirement.

My reference to my own children should in no way imply they were prodigals. They were not. God could not have given two more wonderful children to an undeserving father and mother. God blessed us with the best. That said, I hasten to add that some strategies described in the following pages worked like a charm for us. I won't say which; you'll have to guess!

In these pages you will see children in all shapes and sizes. They vary all over the map in terms of intelligence and energy levels, talents, aptitudes, strengths, weaknesses, temperaments, likes, dislikes, and compliance.

At one end of the compliance continuum we find the highly compliant child devastated by the subtlest look of disapproval.

At the other end is the child hell-bent to do things his or her way. This child defies anyone or anything that tries to offer any direction whatsoever. This child is not automatically a prodigal—as long as the parent understands such a nature and can work effectively with it.

The prodigal comes from a class of pre-defiant children with whom his or her parents get at loggerheads and split apart to opposite sides of a shoving match. Not only will the prodigal then not be taught, he or she will for spite do precisely the opposite of what is expected of him.

Many of the children described in this book are not prodigals. Although the book is about parenting prodigals it is just as much about forms of parenting that will help children never turn prodigal.

We hope these pages will be helpful to the parents of all prodigals. However, for reasons not entirely clear, more than 90 percent of all prodigal children are males.

—S. R. McDill
Tehachapi, California

Introduction

THE MAN WAS RICH, a respected member of his community, a leader. He had two sons. One day his younger son came to him and demanded, "Father, give me my share of your estate now. I don't want to wait until I'm too old to enjoy it."

The father loved both his sons equally and, with sadness, gave the younger son his share to do with as he chose. After all, it wasn't much since the boy was the younger son. Most of his inheritance would go to the older boy. Perhaps he thought his son would show his father's business sense, invest the money, and make a profit. Maybe he believed it would be a learning experience for his son.

Not long after, the young man packed his belongings and set off for new and strange places. He didn't invest the money to make a profit. No. He squandered it in wild youthful abandon, experimenting with wine, women, and song. Naturally there were plenty of people willing to help him spend his money, and soon he was broke.

Unfortunately, this happened about the time a terrible famine descended on the country he was roaming. Times became hard and jobs scarce. All those "friends" who had helped him get rid of his inheritance suddenly could not be found. When his money ran out, so did they. For the first time in his life he felt hunger, loneliness, and fear.

Finally a pig farmer gave him a job. The young man had been raised to believe that pigs were dirty animals that should never be eaten, but hard times called for hard sacrifices. So each day he slopped the pigs. He was so hungry that he even considered eating the pigs' food.

One night, as he lay in the field considering his miserable existence, he thought of home. "My father's servants are treated better than I. They have homes, plenty of food, and don't have to smell pigs all day and night. And here I am, the son of a very successful and well-loved man, starving to death! I'm going home. I know I've messed up and disappointed my dad. I don't deserve to be part of the family anymore. But maybe Dad will give me a job and somewhere to live."

The next morning the young man told the farmer he was quitting, gathered the few possessions he still had, and started toward his own country.

Meanwhile the father had never given up hope that his son would return to his senses and home. Every day he stood on the highest part of his ranch and gazed in the direction he had watched his son go so many months before. One day he saw a small figure that looked familiar.

His heart leaped in his breast. "Can it be?" he whispered. "It looks like my son." He was afraid to get too excited; he'd been disappointed before.

As the figure drew closer the father knew for certain that his boy had come home. Disregarding what his servants might think, he gathered his long garment around him and began to run toward the ragged, dirty, and obviously miserable young man. When he got to his son he threw his arms around him and kissed him.

"Welcome, son, welcome home. I knew you'd come back."

The boy was amazed and humbled. He started to apologize and ask for forgiveness, "Father, I've sinned against heaven and against you. I'm no longer worthy to be called your son."

The father ignored his son's words and called out to his servants, "Bring the best robe and put it on him. Put a ring on his finger and sandals on his feet. Get the fatted calf and kill it. We're going to have a party to celebrate the return of the son I thought was dead."

So they began to celebrate. The prodigal had come home.

This story from the book of Luke (15:11-31, paraphrased) has a happy ending. But not all prodigal stories end as well as this. Actually, there were a few more bitter minutes when the older son came in from the field and found a party in full swing—a party for his rotten little brother who had taken off, squandered his own inheritance, and left him with all the work.

What is a parent supposed to do when the child trained in "the way he should go" does depart radically from it "when he is old"? That's what this book is about.

We give you parenting tips to limit the chance that your child will become a prodigal. These are tips you can apply while your children are still young and innocent.

We also give you practical "what-to-do's" to protect you and your family while you are going through the anguish of living with, or without, the child who has become a prodigal.

Finally, there are things you can do to heal the rift between parents and child. Through implementing them you may entice him home and give the whole family a chance to celebrate and have a party.

Parenting
the
Prodigal

CHAPTER 1

Avoid Creating a Prodigal

WHAT DO YOU SUPPOSE WENT WRONG in the prodigal son's family to compel him to take his share of the fortune and leave home?

Perhaps he was jealous of his older brother who, typical of his culture, got the lion's share of attention as heir to his father's fortune. Perhaps his perfect older brother got under his skin with that never-do-wrong, holier-than-thou attitude. Maybe his father failed to affirm the boy's uniqueness and instill the confidence he needed to develop his own personality and find his own way in the world. Maybe the prodigal was simply rebellious and resented the restrictions he had at home. Or maybe he was a dreamer and an adventurer who wanted to see the outside world.

Whatever the problem, he left parents and home and became a prodigal. Psychologists and family counselors who all too often today hear this type of story can pinpoint certain home situations that tend to influence a child to choose a path leading away from home and parents. What follows is a list of to-do's that may help you avoid creating a prodigal child.

1. Meet your child's legitimate physical needs

This seems so obvious we tend to overlook it. Children need proper food, shelter, safety, security, and physical protection.

Your first task as a parent is to meet the basic physical, biological, psychological, and affectional needs of your children. These are primitive needs that go into the development of their personality. When these needs are not met, a negative emotional reaction takes place in them.

Children cannot meet physical needs by themselves. They will not naturally choose the proper food to eat if left alone. They need to feel that someone genuinely cares about them and is willing and eager to tend to the million and one details of their life, details they cannot articulate, much less take care of. If you neglect to provide proper physical needs your child may—

- Take flight and gravitate to whatever person will provide basic needs in return for services—such as drug-running, solicitation, prostitution.
- Be influenced by groups—such as a cult or gang family—that provide physical needs while teaching wrong values and beliefs.
- Fail to thrive, continually yield to physical illness and develop an attitude that nothing matters.
- Navigate life without a map, wander into treacherous territory, and suffer harm.

2. Provide plenty of emotional support

Create and continually promote a home atmosphere in which your children feel completely cared for. Ingredients of this atmosphere include direct emotional affection and security, tenderness, attachment, bondedness, unconditional love.

Meeting emotional needs is central and vital to healthy personality development. Until children reach roughly mid-teens, they can't meet their own emotional needs. If these needs are not met, children will gravitate toward people who do provide them. Children don't make conscious decisions to select approval sources. They just do. If denied the satisfaction of emotional needs they may—

• Be left with the vague sense that the world is a cold and uncaring place. They may in turn become cold and uncaring themselves.

• Drift toward people who will provide their emotional needs for the wrong reasons.

• Grow up looking for their needs to be met in all the wrong places and through all the wrong means.

• Give up on the world as a caring place and develop an attitude of compensatory meanness.

• Develop an unhealthy hyper-helper personality that drives them to over-serve others and not develop their own burgeoning and unique capabilities, strengths, and assets. They may never find the opportunity—for lack of time and energy—to develop their own personality.

• Develop a flat, dimensionless, lifeless, depressive personality that nothing can animate or energize.

3. Encourage a child's freely chosen interests

Avoid demanding that children be something they are not or do something they cannot. Don't try to make children a clone of yourself or a robot of your choosing; instead encourage them to follow their own talents, aptitudes, and interests.

Children need to find themselves for themselves. All children need encouragement and support in the directions they feel are right for them. Children have a unique set of interests, skills, talents, and competencies which they will intuitively and automatically steer toward unless someone puts up barriers. They need to get involved in and advance in their chosen hobbies and activities.

They can't do this without your help. Denial of your support may cause them to set up a negative emotional reaction toward your expectations and demands so that they—

• Run away from parents and toward those who will encourage and reinforce them in the pathway they intuitively sense is right for them. This pathway could be with prodigal peers who are not safe and wholesome guides.

• Are robbed of discovering that special place they have in this world and the opportunity to experience and develop innate abilities and talents. They never experience the joy that comes from being or doing what they love.

• Become convinced the world is not an exciting place where they will face challenges they can meet. They see the world instead as a place of boring, unexciting chores.

4. Avoid giving too much responsibility too soon

Don't expect children to do more than they are ready

for. Children can't function capably immediately. It takes time to build up their developmental skills. They need positive experiences of success, not failure. Successes lay a solid foundation for developing responsible action. Crack the foundation and the whole building will eventually topple. If this happens children may—

- Take flight.
- Wind up so weighed down that they crumble under the pressure of it all, conclude they are failures, and simply give up.
- Get mad at the world when they find they cannot do what is required of them and set out on a path of rebellion and cynicism.
- Try to do all that is demanded of them but find themselves fumbling. They come to hate themselves and their supposed inabilities and stop trying.

5. Guide with constructive compliments

Avoid mean-spirited criticism without constructive intent or delivery. Such criticism puts children down so they never have a chance to develop the confidence they need to stand on their own feet. Children deprived of positive instruction reinforce their natural self-criticism. They need love which lifts up, not cold belittlement. Children's personalities do not develop through frequent whackings but through gentle and loving guidance. Harsh criticism may—

- Cause them to drift—or sprint!—from your negative influence.
- Lead them to conclude they are general failures in life. Then they may so limit their self-expectations

that they never stretch toward their potential. Instead of growing wings and soaring high, they shrivel and become developmentally stunted.

6. Affirm your child as a person

The home is the right place for a child to be affirmed. The attitude that "children should be seen and not heard" is harmful. Parents must help their children feel they are worthwhile and special. Parents cannot expect schools, churches, sport activities, Boy Scouts, Campfire Girls, or peers properly to affirm a child's identity. Parents need to be the first source of children's awareness of who they are, what they are, and who and what they are to become.

If children do not experience such support they will hunger for it and will turn toward other sources of affirmation. They may—

• Seek role models that are unwholesome but affirm some of their inner needs and ambitions.

• Find or follow agendas that are not good or healthy.

• Develop a permanent inner emptiness that parental affirmation should have filled, becoming candidates for lifetime depression or alienation from others.

• Never develop their own internalized identities but rather experience a wandering, lost, directionlessness, or extreme other-directedness.

7. Encourage free thinking and open expression

How can you guide children properly unless you hear their arguments against what they see as "herd mentality"? Avoid crushing their free-thinking independence with overly harsh parenting.

Some children are, by temperament, free-thinkers, free spirits. This does not become a problem unless parents demand conformity and blind, slavish obedience. When innate creativity and independence are encouraged, cultivated, appreciated, worked with and properly channeled, children will develop responsible, independent functioning. Then you can release them for free flight.

By demanding slavish obedience you may cultivate an angelically demure child that is robbed of the opportunity to operate independently and sprout wings of independence. Children denied opportunity to develop independence may—

• Express independence by overt rebellion (destructive acting out) or by covert rebellion (passive-aggressive mischief making).

• Identify with models who act out rebellion and thus seem heroes because they model what children admire. The children in turn become rebels, using the idealized models as maps.

8. Never abuse your child in any way

As abused children grow up they act out their mistreatment by acting up or shutting down. Eventually society blames such children for what are actually effects of parental abuse.

Parents can have such severe problems of their own that they abuse their children. Defenseless and vulnerable children cannot defend themselves against adults who meet their own disordered needs by abusing them. These defenseless children only react to their world. They cannot create one for themselves. Severely abused children may—

- In extreme circumstances, set up a fantasy world dissociated or cut off from the abuse.
- Internally act out (called "acting in"), which usually manifests in active or passive depression and sometimes suicide.
- Externally act out by serious and pronounced misbehavior at home, school, and community.
- Impersonate (adopt) the actions of the parent inflicting the abuse because they desperately need to counteract the evil power leveled against them.
- Grow up internalizing the wrong values and behaviors, following the pattern of abuse to which they have become accustomed.

9. Maintain harmony in your home
Children need a stable environment that provides safe weather and smooth waters to develop in. They need stable reference points to navigate by. They need stable models and guides to show by example and instruction the path they should follow. Children need stationary limits and boundaries that are like a solid wall they can lean against and rely on. Such stabilities help children internalize equilibrium, constancy, firmness, structuredness, and sureness so they become well-ordered, constant, balanced, and level.

Do not display your own individual or marital problems to such a degree that your good children begin bouncing and spinning out of control as they try to survive and adjust to the craziness or pathology of your behavior. Denial of family and marital tranquillity may cause developing children to—

• Become unbalanced, confused, lost, disordered, chaotic, whipped, shaken up, scrambled in thought and feeling.

• Be unable to make important decisions or to make the wrong decisions as they mature. This will prevent them from taking those secure steps required to move them into the next developmental phase.

• Never find anything they consider real or solid. Everything remains in disorder, turmoil, and turbulence, including themselves.

• Give up on life as being anything but constant pain. They will give up the idea that they can be effectual. Rather they will live a sadly passive existence, reacting to events in a disorganized way.

• Lack reliable internal reference points developed within themselves. They will grope blindly and dumbly for reference points outside themselves until they find some—probably the wrong ones.

• Learn firsthand what unstable behavior looks like and to follow their parents' behaviors, modes, and ways of thinking. Then they unwittingly treat their own children as pathologically as their parents did them.

10. Teach by example, not crippling punishment

Heavy-handed punishment generally comes from reactive parental anger. Punishing from anger first scares children, then sets up in them a reactive counter-anger they dare not openly express. Parental anger also teaches children how to avoid further painful collisions by not doing whatever they were doing but does not tell children what they *should* do.

Parents should give their children maps of routes to follow, highways to take, and roadblocks to avoid. Directions that tell only where *not* to go do not tell children where *to* go. Children don't come already equipped with a working understanding of actions and attitudes. They have to be taught, shown, guided, and patiently instructed.

Angry parenting is like putting children into a complex airplane cockpit and telling them to fly without showing them how, then hitting them every time they make a mistake. It is unlikely such children will get the airplane airborne. Rather they will get so nervous they won't be able to think or function at all. Or they will get so angry they will tell their instructor off and leave the cockpit.

Heavy-handed, crippling punishment almost always brings about tragic results such as—

• Causing children to express anger covertly or passive-aggressively in destructive ways. This deprives the punishing parent of constructive influence needed to implant positive values.

• Crushing and traumatizing them so they seek to escape. Parents then lose their position of nearness, which is needed to influence children constructively and effectively.

• Closing their mind toward anything parents say from then on, depriving them of receptive soil in which the information they are taking in can be nourished.

• Estranging them from parents and forcing them

into the protection of others whose ways they ought not adopt.

• Forcing them rebelliously to adopt positions that are opposite to what parents hope for. Children desperately need a feeling of strength, so they set themselves up to punch back. Had the parent not punched the child in the first place, the child would feel no need to punch back.

By adopting an "oh-yeah!" stance, children are lost to any guidance parents might try to offer. Thereafter children are on their own in a world full of danger, unequipped to find the right path by themselves. They will flounder around until "effective (and probably unhealthy) others" nurture them.

11. Overcome your own surliness or bullishness

To children, an attitude of "you can't mess with me" looks like the essence of awe-inspiring power. Other adults will see this behavior as tragicomic, cocky, pompous, or pathetic power-mongering. To children this attitude may seem something to internalize and play back with a high-struttin' swagger that makes them feel equal to any adult.

After all, "Dad is strong and pushy and sometimes combative (obnoxious, really). If it works for him, it'll work for me. What's good enough for Dad is good enough for me." Such children thus—

• Become uneducable to the ways of true adult maturity.

• Wind up alienating healthy, gentle, fair-minded peers. They attract those who seek the trappings, spoils, and ways of power.

- Learn the hard way that such snotty traits do not work for healthy relationships. Before long, they wind up alone in lonely, bitter cynicism.

- As a result of mimicking and thus adopting certain brattish parental qualities, such as petulance or insolence, children invite painful collisions between themselves and equally childish parents. This leads to painful, juvenile shoving matches of contrary wills between parent and child. Of course, children lose because they are forever one-down with respect to the powers of parents.

- Never learn the valuable and venerable arts of dialogue, persuasion, and graceful compromise. These are learned primarily through long-term reverential observation, careful and respectful rehearsal, painstaking practice, and slow absorption.

12. Watch your own attitude toward authority

Sometimes parents are what I call "closet rebels." Their rebellion is apparent only to those who live close to them. Even family members, however, may not see the problem because closet rebels seem so convincingly conventional. They may be highly successful in life and career and come across to the general public as smooth, with great aristocratic flair and polish. But inwardly closet rebels hold cynical attitudes and are scornful of almost everything and everyone they encounter or experience.

Seeing parents as strong and powerful, children may sense and be impressed by the rebellion. Children may see the traits of closet rebels as grown-up, adult behavior. They may adopt that disdainful, superiority-based scornfulness and a swaggering, strutting, sneering, adolescent caricature of it. This may make it impossible to educate or train them in the ways of maturity.

Parents grieve for such children because they are wasting precious adolescence fighting all who might help them grow up. The parents wonder how in the world the children got so negative. All the while they are blind to the fact that one or both of them, through modeling, taught their child how to be supercilious, contemptuous, and disdainful, attitudes that can turn the adolescent into the prodigal.

Internal Problems of Children

As we will explore in future chapters, there is a time for all parents to face how they may have contributed to a child's failures. But guilt can be overdone. If you are suddenly overwhelmed with your own load of undeserved guilt, read on.

Ted was headed for trouble from the time he hit puberty. He was an angel, mostly, until his twelfth birthday. Then something went seriously wrong. He started doing drugs, all he could get his hands on. He didn't seem to care how they might affect him long-term; he just wanted excitement and to be "cool."

Ted's appearance grew grungier and grungier. He wore overlarge jeans low slung around a shrinking waist. His vocabulary changed from a wholesome, excited, spontaneous, constant chatter to monosyllabic grunts or profanities too offensive to repeat.

His parents went crazy trying to control him, but he wouldn't be reined in. Some of their friends advised them to let go and let Ted suffer his own consequences. Others just fretted and wrung their hands, not knowing what to suggest. The parents went to therapists to see what they had done to create such a monster. Ted went with them once or twice, then stopped. He didn't need that.

After a while his parents began to realize that they had not necessarily done anything wrong. Besides, it was better to try to figure out what to do now, to focus their energy on the future rather than trace back the chain of cause and effect leading to this crisis. Finding historical cause and effect connections often reveal more about the analysts and their theories than about what really happened on the road to ruin. The parents were not avoiding responsibility, they were just beginning to realize that all sorts of things influence kids, not just parental wrongs.

Perhaps you have provided the best parenting you were able to. You never deliberately withheld the physical, biological, moral, and spiritual support your child needed. You gently followed the admonition to "train a child in the way he should go," yet he did "turn from it." What other possibility could there be for his rebellion?

Some children have internal problems that happen on their own, without your help, and make for prodigal acting out. These problems may be discussed under three broad categories, including—

1. Genetic inheritance or endowment (biological predisposition known as one's basic temperament) in which children are strong-willed, contrary, perhaps insolent.

2. Biologically determined temperament of seeking excitement (adrenalin addiction) in a world of rules. By breaking these rules, children experience cheap thrills and tumultuous free-for-all, cops-and-robbers chases.

3. Biologically determined hyperactivity which parents cannot effectively handle. Common methods of discipline that would work with non-hyperactive children do not work with hyperactive ones. Such punishment as spanking (which generally becomes more severe when parents discover it isn't working), sitting in the corner, grounding, and so forth, fail to modify hyperactive children's behavior. Other methods are needed.

Coping with a Prodigal

No parent wants to create a prodigal, nor does any parent intentionally choose to suffer through the multi-year agony of housing or maintaining one. Fortunately, there are ways to solve prodigal child problems and find your way out of the prodigal thicket. Here are three immediate suggestions if you and your family are being torn asunder by a difficult child.

First, take care of yourself, your life, your non-prodigal loved ones. Declare time out from dealing with your prodigal. Find a balance between focusing on activities that refresh and restore versus those that strain and drain. Be sure to refresh and renew yourself. Your whole life cannot be centered on dealing with problems, otherwise you risk burnout, depression, and cynicism.

Second, deal directly, objectively, non-emotionally, philosophically, and without self-accusation with the problems your prodigal brings home. Remind yourself that his problems are his. The fallout of his behavior is now—or could become—your problem. Yet you can aim to remain calm and serenely detached. Treat your prodigal as though he were someone else's child.

Don't berate, implore, make deals. Such strategies don't work. Release his problems back to him. Let him sweat them; why should you? Protect yourself from the consequences of his misadventures, possibly even through legal emancipation proceedings before he reaches age eighteen. Let him—rather than you—grow gray and haggard. Remain warm, open, and loving, but learn to let go as quickly as you can. Your sanity demands it.

Third, continually remind yourself of the first suggestion. Take care of yourself, your life, and your nonprodigal loved ones.

The following chapters will help you deal in more depth with strategies for coping with a prodigal or worry that your child is headed in a prodigal direction.

CHAPTER 2

Never Give Up on Your Prodigal!

PETER EPITOMIZED EVERY PARENT'S nightmare. He instinctively knew how to do exactly the opposite of what his parents—and everyone else—wanted him to do. Year after year Mom and Dad suffered through complaints from school, police, their church, his friends' parents, neighbors. Whoever Peter came in contact with would eventually call his parents to take Peter home because he was causing trouble.

Peter wound up in continuation school because regular classroom teachers would have nothing to do with him. This didn't bother Peter; he wanted nothing to do with them either. Finally Peter quit school, bummed around, and continued to give his parents grief. He experimented with drugs and alcohol, picked fights, and was hauled off to jail for various minor offenses.

Early in Peter's life, however, his parents had resolved never to give up hope. And despite Peter's evident lack of response, that resolve showed through their grief, anger, and embarrassment. As Peter continued to get into one scrape after another his parents at times felt like strangling him. But somehow they always turned their negative feelings around to more positive ones, and their hope never faded. They found strength to parent from love, hope, and good faith.

Peter sensed, at some deep level, that his parents loved him in spite of himself. This knowledge kept him close to them even through the tough times when his parents were so angry they could hardly speak to him.

Eventually their resolve paid off. The demons that drove Peter gradually left. His parents' hope was vindicated.

Peter's parents could easily have written him off to go his prodigal way, resentful that he had no one but himself and his coterie of troublemakers. His world could have consisted of negative influencers who could have sealed his destiny. His life could have been one of cynicism, bitterness, troublemaking, and unhappiness for himself and all he touched. And he would have had no one to blame but himself.

Peter's parents probably never sat down to map out the path they were to follow, but they gave him four things he could get no other way. They gave him hope; faith in his essential goodness; optimism that there is something good about the world; and confidence that he was loved, cherished, and forgiven.

No matter what trouble Peter made or stumbled into, these qualities eventually turned him around and stood him on a higher ground.

The "Tough Love" Approach

For a while "tough love" seemed a solution to exhausted parents of acting-out teens. This approach stressed that a dose of straight, raw reality would be like shock treatment, so shaking up children that they would straighten up, grow up, get in line. The basic idea was that parents had to let their rebellious kids experience the natural consequences of their rebellion. Such hard lessons, it was thought and taught, were the only way mavericks and rebels learned. Step aside, parents. Let natural consequences take their toll.

Parents were not to give in to their natural tendency to rescue, not to feel pulled in, not to soften reality's blows. Indeed, there was a compelling and seductive logic to the notion of natural consequences, so much so that a whole generation of parents were coached to step back, let go, and watch their kids get jolted into reality and, hopefully, into maturity by the natural, painful outcomes of their (mis)adventures.

Sadly, there had not been credible research to support the basic notion that natural consequences taught lessons to prodigal children, any more than prison teaches convicts not to break the law. There were only often-told anecdotes or testimonies describing the lucky exception rather than the rule. Nor was there appreciation that some consequences themselves are so damaging that they don't teach. Rather, they overwhelm, overcome, crush, cripple. Some consequences irreparably destroy.

We take a non-tough-love stand in this book. We believe parents need to be accessible and tirelessly ready to approach and be approached. They need to pursue and interfere and intervene for all they are worth (but in the right ways). They need to send a clear message of vigorous action-oriented love and concern and unflagging commitment to their job of ushering their kids safely into adulthood. Parents of prodigal children need to follow the example of the loving father in the parable of the prodigal.

The lesson of that parable was not about parenting but about homecoming, reunion, and rejoicing. We need to be careful not to draw the wrong moral from a parable, or to stretch and bend it to include a lesson not there. Had the parable been about quality parenting it would have portrayed the father saying an emphatic no to the son's shocking (and insulting) request that he receive his inheritance early. The father would have seen in the son's request immaturity and irresponsibility and would not have entrusted the inheritance to him.

Sometimes a prodigal is so upsetting to the whole family that parents must take steps to protect the other members, lest they all become troubled. But a child must know that he is loved, no strings attached, with a truly unconditional love.

No one ever said parenting would be a picnic. It isn't. In the best of times parenting will be an intensive, time-consuming project, with precious little relief between duty calls. While your child is making one mistake after another, getting into scrape after scrape, you will find it necessary to maintain a mind-set that features hope, faith, optimism, and confidence.

The Roles of Hope, Faith, Optimism, Confidence

Anne Frank said, "In spite of everything I still think at heart people are basically good." This statement reflects hope, faith, optimism, and confidence.

Hope is believing that what we want to happen will eventually happen, that everything will eventually work itself out and end up okay. Such an attitude allows you to avoid getting so discouraged that you abandon your child when he needs you the most. Even though your child is willing to throw you away as so much useless interference, you need to maintain a spirit of "I'm still with you, kid." And you need to demonstrate that spirit when it's not easy or immediately or palpably felt.

Faith is something you place in your child whether earned or not. Your child may be failing miserably, but faith is a buoying power, a flotation device, that keeps things from getting too heavy when they are looking really bad. Hope is something you establish in yourself that stays with you, guiding and orienting you in right ways toward your prodigal. Faith, on the other hand, is something you lodge in your child.

Faith has a two-party influence effect. Faith affects you as you lodge it in your child, and faith influences your child. Children feel your faith powerfully in the way you look at them. They feel it forcefully in your body language.

"I believe in you . . ." comes through in myriads of little ways. Such faith becomes a powerful, invisible force-field within which your child lives and breathes and gains an overall sense of self.

Optimism takes the most hopeful view of matters

and expects the best outcome in any circumstances. While the prodigal is busy moving from one misadventure to another, optimism will help his parents discipline themselves to see beyond the mess into the aspirations of the child and focus on those. The prodigal does not necessarily want to be identified with his messes or have his nose rubbed in them. The wise mom and dad look to what the prodigal hopes to accomplish. They recognize it in much the same way they praised the unrecognizable finger painting their child presented for acclaim as a preschooler.

Confidence believes in one's own or in another's abilities. All children, prodigal or not, hunger for someone to believe in them. They will work themselves to death for it and will accordingly be deeply influenced by whoever places confidence in them. Confidence affects both the one who finds it and shows it *and* the one who receives it.

As you place yourself in a self-created, confidence-based mind-set toward your child, this confidence helps you to see, select, and reinforce the more praiseworthy aspects of your child's behavior. When you are poised (or more accurately, when you deliberately poise yourself) to attend to the praiseworthy, you tend to overlook the less than praiseworthy as inconsequential or a fluke.

Conversely, when you shift to a critical mind-set toward your prodigal, you poise yourself to attend primarily to the bad. Thus you will not see what is good as it plays out around you. You become selectively blinded.

You control your lens. You can change it.

The Power of Self-Fulfilling Prophecies

We hear a lot about self-fulfilling prophecies. "Name it and claim it" evangelism loudly demands it; self-improvement courses emphatically proclaim it; sales conferences enthusiastically trumpet it.

Self-fulfilling prophecies have a number of ingredients. They are systems of good or bad expectations, beliefs, or feelings about reality. They are compelling, gripping, and intense. They shape perceptions or actions in such a way as to bring into being what is expected.

We experience what we expect to experience. When we have a strong feeling—good or bad—about something or someone, including ourselves, we are inescapably and unavoidably shaped by these feelings without being aware of it. Our feelings about our self shape how we view our self. Our feelings about our mate shape how we view her or him. And our feelings about our children shape how we view them, for good or bad. We cannot escape, however hard we may try, the gripping, shaping, guiding influence of feelings.

When we have powerful expectations or beliefs about life, we're deeply and invisibly affected by them. For example, if we deeply fear that something bad is going to happen, whether or not it really does, we unconsciously weave that fear into our perceptions, interpret reality in terms of it, and thus experience it. The invisible hands of beliefs, feelings, expectations, and fears move everyone around in ways that can turn good people into monsters and, happily, monsters back into good people.

Moms and dads who are otherwise good parents

may shift gears when their expectations for their children turn sour. All it takes is one fear, negative belief, or expectation with enough punch, and these parents pause and turn, feeling-wise, against their child.

But we do not have to be victims of our beliefs, fears, and expectations. All of us can consciously control our belief systems. It takes no magic, just discipline. And it is on this particular discipline—no other —that each case turns.

Carver was the small-town high school football star, with a 3.5 grade point average. He and a friend arrived early at a friend's party. No one answered the front door, so the two boys started around to the back, thinking everyone was in the backyard. One neighbor saw the two teenagers going through the side gate. Noting that Carver was African-American, the neighbor called police.

When the police arrived at the party, which was indeed in the backyard, they drew their guns on Carver. They hauled all partygoers (no parents were on the scene) to the police station and cited them. But Carver was treated differently. The police were going to send him to juvenile hall. Fortunately the other teenagers and some parents who had arrived at the station stood up for Carver. The police finally let the boy go.

The neighbor who had called the law had recently moved to the small community from a big city where racial tension was a major problem. He assumed that an African-American kid "sneaking" through a side gate was up to no good. He experienced what he expected to experience. But he was wrong.

Scott was the kind of preacher's kid most preachers

hope for—head of the youth group, great with people. He got good grades and was almost elected homecoming king.

Being a normal curious kid, Scott wanted to find out what was so exciting about drugs. (Statistics reveal that a large percentage of high school kids try drugs at least once.) After the homecoming game, Scott went to a party with friends and tried marijuana for the first time. The joint found its way around the group. Everyone inhaled deeply, tried to hold in the smoke where it was supposed to do its magic, and coughed and gagged.

Everyone got high all right, but not from the pot. Their high came from hyperventilation and the orthostatic hypotension that accompanies it. (This is the feeling that comes from standing up too fast and almost passing out as blood rushes from the brain.) Scott tried to feel the effect he'd heard so much about but didn't. This is not unusual for first-timers.

Later that evening he tried again. This time he felt the drug effect but was not impressed. He decided marijuana was overrated and had no appeal for him.

Unfortunately, someone called the local sheriff, who descended on the scene with his deputies and swept all the teenagers into custody. *What a coup!* thought the locals. *Look at these misbehaving kids. We'll make an example of them!* They did. They made a public spectacle of the sweep.

Scott had his share of publicity, as did his parents. His folks were humiliated and indignant. Suddenly they saw Scott not as a bright, decent kid with a good future (who deserved to have this caper eventually dismissed) but as a no-good rebel. Their perspective on him switched instantly from positive to negative.

So did their ways of interacting with their son. They looked at him in an entirely different light and defined him in that light. They saw only those behaviors that could be interpreted as negative. Nothing Scott did from then on was good enough.

This was a huge mistake. Scott had smoked parts of two joints—hardly proof of a criminal mind. Yet that was precisely how he was treated—as a criminal.

After much time of being interpreted in a negative way, Scott saw that he could not win; he gave up trying to prove he was not a bad kid. Rejected from the community of the righteous, he found welcome in the only other community left, that of the unrighteous.

His family was convinced he was gone, especially his preacher dad who needed to distance himself from his son's misadventures to save his own hide. He launched a series of sermons on the wages of sin, with his son as the main object lesson. By now the community at large saw Scott as a loser and treated him as such. The effect was to cement Scott deeper into his community of no-goods, until he became their leader.

One small, insignificant event that should have been shrugged off as so much youthful curiosity turned into a soul-branding experience with tragic consequences.

Parents who can steadily discipline their minds into positive channels when they interact with their prodigal kids can turn negative children around. But it takes time and infinite patience. And inexhaustible consistency.

We see ourselves as others see us. At the turn of the century, Thomas Horton Cooley developed the idea that all children form a notion about who they are on the basis of how others interact with them. As children grow up, this notion continues to expand. If other people interact positively with children, they adopt a friendly attitude toward themselves. Conversely, if others treat them in an unfriendly way, they develop an equally unfriendly attitude toward themselves. The friendly attitude toward oneself we label as "positive self-esteem." An unfriendly attitude is "low self-esteem."

As children (and adults too) form their self-concepts, they do so on the basis of reflected appraisals. That is, children sense intuitively how others look at them, whether appreciatively or critically. They store these mini-impression "messages" into banks that store summary impressions. Since they don't have the mental sophistication to edit negative impressions, they just store all messages as inherently true information about themselves.

As these impressions pile up over time, children weigh the positive against the negative. The scale tips in the direction of whichever carries the most weight. The result is that they see themselves as appreciated, valued, good—or as unappreciated, devalued, bad. Every contact children have with others adds to this reflection of themselves seen in the eyes of others as if in a mirror—hence the description, "looking-glass self."

If we realize that this process continues unendingly throughout life, we can use it to our children's advantage. By consciously projecting positive messages through our verbal and nonverbal interactions with our children, and by neutralizing any negative messages they receive from others, we can deliberately construct, message by message, a positive view of self in each child.

Here's where discipline enters again. By carefully monitoring our own feelings toward our children, and by making deliberate decisions about eliminating "bad child" messages and consistently transmitting "attaboy, attagirl" ones, we create good children. Children, being human, respond to our warm positiveness toward them with warmth and positiveness toward us. This establishes an important mutual linkage that keeps us and our children positively bonded. That's what healthy parenting is all about.

We filter everything we experience through a mind-set. A mind-set is a personal way of looking at things. Mind-sets are infinitely subtle navigational systems. They are made up of our deeply personal attitudes, beliefs, expectations, likes, dislikes, values, fears, hopes, aspirations, defeats. Everything that goes into making us who we are goes into our mind-set.

Why is this important to understand? Because people tend to believe that what they see is objectively real and unchangeable. We tend to believe that everyone sees things the same way—the way we do. Nothing could be further from the truth. What we "see" gets carefully and thoroughly filtered through our perceptual sieves. Not everything gets through, only what is in harmony with our basic beliefs about ourselves and life.

Once we recognize that everything we perceive

and do is largely controlled by our personal mind-set, we can begin to carefully assess what is in it. It's like knowing what's in a navigational system so we can use it more competently. When we understand the inner workings of our navigation system, we can remove the bugs and recalibrate more accurately. When we know what our blind spots are and how they control every decision we make, we can remove them and see more clearly.

Most important, we can reprogram our mind-set, permitting it to be more constructive and positive. We can reshape our thought patterns into more useful configurations. These improved mind-sets can guide us better and help us do our parenting jobs properly, or at least better.

The Pull of Approval, Acceptance, Validation

Everyone, prodigals included, is subject to the psychological pushes and pulls of human nature. Your prodigal wants the same things everyone else wants, emotionally speaking. We all need and want approval, acceptance, and validation from others. We will automatically gravitate toward sources that provide these needs. Like heliotropic plants that turn their flower heads toward and follow the sun throughout the day, people fixate on sources of emotional warmth and nourishment and follow those sources wherever they go.

We also automatically return warmth for warmth. And the converse is true—coldness begets coldness. When those who are close to us do not react warmly toward us, we feel released to turn toward other sources of warmth to fix on and follow.

If you understand this psychological truth, you can use it to your prodigal's advantage. That takes discipline and perseverance, however; it won't work magic overnight. By systematically showing approval, acceptance, and validation of your prodigal's lost and hungry inner self (not the rebellious, angry outer self as shown in his or her actions), you place yourself in the position of becoming your child's source of influence. You become the agent who actively feeds and nourishes your prodigal emotionally. You become the one your child fixes upon and follows.

Then you can lead by warm loving example, not by preaching or lecturing, which estranges and alienates. You can trust that the invisible hand of emotional hunger will gently and surely pull your prodigal back into the healthy pathways you want your child to walk.

It won't happen overnight, count on it. But in many cases it will happen. As heliotropes follow the sun, so will your prodigal feel enticed to follow you.

The Destructive Power of Criticism and Condemnation

Just as approval, acceptance, and validation cultivate warmth, criticism and condemnation cultivate coldness. Remember the last critical and condemning person you associated with. You will probably note that criticism and condemnation not only alienate, they also remove from your developing child the building blocks the child needs to construct a solid foundation for later building. Children need plentiful amounts of emotional nourishment to develop well and with psychological solidness. They cannot mature in an atmosphere that is devoid of elements that nourish and strengthen.

Criticism crushes. Condemnation strips children of initiative, autonomy, industry, competency, mastery, confidence. Children need these qualities as surely as they need oxygen, food, and water. Without them they shrivel and die. Without them children will quickly turn away from your presence—therefore, your influence. They will seek what you should be providing from someone else and possibly a wrong source. Then you lose all opportunity to be the agent who influences them in the right direction.

Remember, leading and guiding are done most effectively by attracting, not pushing. Children, however, must feel that they are free agents, even in choosing whether to turn toward the warmth of caring. They thus avoid a shameful sense of dependence on parents.

CHAPTER 3

Encourage Uniqueness

NO MATTER HOW MANY CHILDREN you have, each is different. No two are exactly alike, even identical twins. No children fall into a category. They are not generic anythings. They are persons with unique attributes, skills, abilities, talents, strengths—and yes, weaknesses, just like you.

Suppose someone were to decide who you are according to a single negative trait, ignoring all your good points and categorizing you according to subjective evaluation, sticking a label on you, shoving you into a predetermined pigeonhole. You would bristle, feel demeaned and insulted, and probably rebel. Children are even more sensitive to being classified and defined by someone else.

Many parents, however, probably influenced by media hype of teenagers who stray and follow the "pied pipers" of gangs, drugs, rebellion, and general meanness, tend to interpret every nonconforming action of their own children as the beginning of prodigalism. When you struggle regularly with a difficult son or daughter, it is tempting and almost automatic to type your child according to what you fear in "bad" kids.

When your child does not fit categories with which you are familiar, your mind automatically, due to ancient instincts, focuses on what you think is twisting her or him away from your predetermined plan. You lump your child into the category of people you identify as defiant. You pick up on anything that is contrary to what you see as "normal." You focus on long hair, short hair, Mohawk; on loud, undecipherable (to you) music; on "weird" clothing; on all the things every youth culture adopts to show uniqueness and which parents view as sending their children to hell in a handbasket.

Yet ten years from now what will it matter? Even the wildest and most revolting radicals of the sixties, when the shock value of their behavior subsided, grew up, settled down, cut their hair. Few radicals from the sixties are still around today. The majority entered their thirties and went corporate with three-piece suits, briefcases, the works.

Many parents kill their relationship with their teenagers because of a passing phase. These parents want to control their children's behavior, which teenagers hate. How can you avoid stereotyping your child? How can you see a child as a unique person? It isn't easy.

Don't Label Your Child
Generalizing causes you to focus on a single trait (the "most salient characteristic," the literature calls it) and magnify it until it mushrooms in your mind, becoming much larger than it is in reality. But people are made up of many traits—some good, some bad. If only one

trait, a negative one, grabs your attention, you tend to ignore the positive traits. You magnify the negative completely out of proportion. You wind up defining and labeling your child on the basis of that single "offensive" trait.

That's not fair, appropriate, or a way of enhancing the relationship between you and your child. When you interpret a child's values, motives, actions, and beliefs only in negative terms, and display your disapproval on the basis of your perception, you begin a self-perpetuating process that can become a negative self-fulfilling prophecy. Whatever label you tack onto your child traps both you and your child in that configuration, true or not.

In *The Presentation of Self in Everyday Life* (Doubleday, 1959), Erving Goffman speaks of the "funnel of betrayal" that occurs when two or more people interact with each other toward a third person on the basis of a single selected negative feature (the "salient characteristic"). Before long, nothing else about that third person matters, gets noticed, or is even responded to. Only the highlighted negative feature attracts attention. After a while the "bad" feature becomes the victim's label.

Labeling results in automatically interacting with your child on the basis of the label. If the label has quite a sting to it for you, your reaction will be even stronger and your interactions with your child more negative. When a prodigal notices your label, he may react in one of several ways. He may fight you on its accuracy. He may buy into the label and act it out more and more intensely just to spite you. Or he may like and accept the label as his identity.

Children are sensitive to labels, so much so that often they conform to the label tacked on them by parents or others. The label becomes familiar to them and, as they see it, expected of them. They do not have to wear the label, which didn't even exist before the two or more people decided informally among themselves the kind of persons they are. So labeled children walk a pathway they did not select, did not make, and probably don't want to walk.

Sticking a negative label on your child will gain nothing but will lose a lot. A negative label effectively eclipses everything else about your child. All the positives are overlooked.

As a parent you should learn who the whole child is, bypass the negatives, and cultivate, encourage, and develop his positives. In passing only you may comment on the negative. But then, unless it's dangerous, let it go. (We'll comment later on handling of dangerous negatives). If you battle over negatives, your child's positive attributes may never develop. Rather, your child will abandon his or her positives just to rub your nose in the identified painful negative quality.

Don't Jump to Conclusions

Jake was a high-spirited teenager who enjoyed all the exciting things high school had to offer—except his Spanish class. He was doing awful in Spanish. The midterm was coming up, and he knew if he didn't make a C he would lose his place on the swimming team. So he asked an adult friend to help him study. They worked hard the whole weekend before the test, and Jake got an A! Totally unheard of for Jake.

Meanwhile it was discovered that someone had stolen the test answers. The teacher notified the principal and several of the youth were called into his office. Some of those who got better than expected grades admitted they had bought the test from someone but would not tell who.

Because Jake's grade was the biggest surprise, everyone assumed he was the one who stole the test answers. Jake's friend was out of town and was the only one who could clear his name. Jake was threatened with expulsion. Things looked bleak. In a few days, though, the friend returned to town and cleared Jake's name.

Johnny, fifteen, a high school track student, went into the boys' restroom right after one of the better-known drug-using kids had used it. A passing teacher smelled something funny and went in to investigate. There stood Johnny washing his hands and face, marijuana smoke still wafting about the room. The teacher collared Johnny and hauled him to the principal's office.

It wasn't the first time Johnny had been in the principal's office; he'd had a couple of run-ins before, for minor problems. But since the principal had been under fire from the community due to several incidents of drug abuse among high school kids, he searched Johnny. He didn't find any condemning evidence but called the police, who called Johnny's parents.

Wanting to be recognized for doing something about the "drug problem," the principal made a big noise about the incident. Everybody was surprised and horrified—the public, Johnny's friends, his family, and Johnny himself. The only thing they had against Johnny was that he was in the room with the smoke. But that was enough. It didn't matter how much Johnny protested, there was enough evidence to create doubt in his parents' minds. Besides, they had feared such a thing for a while now. After all, they read the papers and watched TV.

Johnny stood exposed, feeling rejected and spurned by everyone he had depended on and related to. Before long, he got tired of trying to defend himself. He felt lonely, angry, bitter, and cynical enough to drop out of school.

Then he did what dropouts often do. He hung out with other dropouts. The dropout crowd tends to take in all comers, the badder the better. They reinforce a rather nasty, cynical, view of life. Johnny came under the spell of a charismatic leader who took him under his wing and educated him into the ways of the counterculture. Johnny became a prodigal.

As this kind of story typically goes, that could have been the end of Johnny. He did walk the prodigal path for a time. However, before he became permanently fixed in the ways of crime, he miraculously (whether through his own self-concern and pride, or through the prayers of someone who cared for him) extricated himself from his counterculture. He moved out of his situation to a place where he could begin fresh, where nobody knew about his brief brush with the law, and where he could begin to build his own confidence and trust in others again.

This story should have taken a different direction. Early in the scenario the principal—and Johnny's parents—could have considered the many factors sur-rounding Johnny. No marijuana was found on John-ny's person or in his locker. He had never been known to try drugs. And other than prankishness in class Johnny had been a good student.

Don't Emphasize One Feature Over Others

Cartoonists pencil humorous drawings that highlight some distinct feature they are caricaturing. They en-large it or give it some compelling twist or distortion. They add a comic or, in the case of political cartoons, insulting dimension. These drawings are meant to be humorous, laughed at.

When you caricature your child—select one fea-ture and blow it out of proportion—you reduce his or her fullness and substance to one dimension. The re-sults are certainly not funny to your child and eventu-ally not to you.

When you live with cartoons of a child as though they were true likenesses, you never see your mistake. Along with the mental cartoons come an instanta-neous and compelling sense that your perceptions are accurate.

This sense of accuracy prevents your feeling the need to check whether your beliefs about your child are rooted in reality. It never occurs to you that your mental picture of your child may be unfairly and dis-proportionately skewed toward the negative. You nev-er think to step outside your subjective frame of refer-ence and take a second look at your child from anoth-er, more objective perspective.

Misperceiving, misinterpreting, and misunderstanding your child by seeing only his or her cartoon traps both of you in a no-win situation.

Become Soul-Connected with Your Child

Since you were the one who categorized, labeled, and caricatured your child, he or she is not responsible to change the situation. You are. How do you wipe the canvas clean and start over?

Your child needs to feel soul-connected with someone who offers understanding and nurturing. You, through positive ground-setting, could be that person. Soul-connectedness occurs when you have a positive relationship with your child, an actual relationship tangibly felt, valued, and cherished.

CHAPTER 4

It's Okay to Be an Authority, but Not Authoritarian

CHILDREN EVENTUALLY must seek their own counsel. This development is normal and appropriate and must happen if they are to become whole, independent, productive members of society. How successful they are depends a great deal on the style of parenting they have received. And remember, the goal of parenting is to work yourself out of a job.

There are three broad types of parenting—permissive, authoritarian, and authoritative.

A permissive parent says, "I am I, and you are you. I am not in this world to live up to your expectations, nor are you here to live up to mine. I found my way, you can find yours."

Permissive parenting produces children who tend to be lost. They wander, sometimes aimlessly, looking for guideposts or guides to help them find their way. Permissive parents are far too lenient. They allow their child to flop and flounder, guaranteeing a formlessness with no internal skeleton of values and structures that give form and shape to the body as it fleshes out.

The authoritarian parent says, "I'm the boss. You'll do as I say because I say it. Case closed." An authoritarian parent is far too harsh, forcing mindless and slavish obedience. An authoritarian denies children the room they need to sprout wings and try them out in safe airspace. The authoritarian parent dictates and keeps children so close they have no space for free flight. The authoritarian style cramps and discourages the exercise and development of independent thinking.

The authoritarian's children take one of two paths. They learn not to think, allowing parents—and other authority figures—to do all their thinking for them. Or they resist, covertly or overtly, and take control of their own flight through rebellion.

A third type of parent is authoritative. This parent says, "Okay, guys, here's the plan. Here's why we have this particular plan." Then the parent follows up by explaining, at the child's level of understanding, why it has to be this way. Even though this parent prescribes the plan, he or she remains open to answering questions, often incorporating amendments.

When the authoritative parent's child objects or disobeys, the authoritative parent says, "Whoa, little dogie, the trail's over here, and here's why you must stay on it." The authoritative parent then gives another description of the plan's logic while affirmatively steering the child back on course, perhaps making minor adjustments in the overall plan to accommodate the child's wishes and needs.

Perhaps you started out wrong. But it's not too late

to redirect your parenting style. With effort you can turn things around.

Avoid Being Hypercritical

We do not trust the person who says, "Do as I say, not as I do." Children learn early to internalize what they experience more than what they are told. They try to take in and become what they see around them—good or bad, regardless of what you say to them.

Parents who exemplify, at home as well as in public, the qualities they want their children to follow, find their children following in their footsteps. Children internalize your powerful silent sermons on honesty, for example, when they see you return the extra dollar the cashier accidentally gave you in change.

Allow Your Children to Make Mistakes

Student pilots learn as much or more from bad landings than good ones. But they should never define themselves in terms of bad landings. Bad landings are to be gotten out of their system during training flights. That's what training flights are for. Eventually student pilots make fewer bad landings and are considered good pilots according to their own and others' definition. But the label "good pilot" comes only after all their mistakes have been worked out of their system.

Unless we are slow maturers or mentally challenged, we all form by eighteen a rough working sense of self. We form that working idea we carry in the forefront of our thinking that describes who and what we are in life. That basic, roughly hewn idea of who we are guides us to select people, places, things, and experiences in harmony with our sense of self. We retain what fits, repeat the experience, and drop whatever does not fit. These experiences—good and bad—encountered throughout childhood and adolescence, form a working sense of self like colored pieces of tile form a complete mosaic.

Experience falls into two categories: ego-syntonic or ego-dystonic. An ego-syntonic experience is in harmony with what you feel fits or suits you well. An ego-dystonic experience is one that makes you cringe when you experience or remember it. Along the way we make countless mistakes. We bless those who look the other way and don't make a big deal over the experience. How good it feels when our golf partner, after we just sliced the ball over two fairways, says, "That doesn't count. Take a mulligan on that one."

Similarly our teenagers appreciate us when we good-naturedly tell them to "take a mulligan" after they botch something. As a parent you should strategically turn away from your teenager's mistakes, which are better forgotten. Children cringe, suffer, and punish themselves enough without your reinforcing their discomfort.

We all try for all we are worth to erase from memory things that make us cringe. Children should be allowed the luxury of forgetting those humiliating times when they feel the whole world is staring or laughing at them. As long as their children learn from the experience, wise and gracious parents will allow the process of forgetting (erasing) to have its desired effect in their teenagers. With the residue erased, the teenager can get on with the process of retaining the good and getting beyond the bad.

By picking and choosing what is kept and what is erased from memory, teenagers assemble for them-selves a composite picture of who and what they are. Graciously allow your teenager the priceless luxury of undisturbed erasing. You do this best by not rubbing their nose in mistakes. Criticism of mistakes makes learners freeze up and choke. They feel like taking flight from or quickly covering up messes. No one wants to stand in the spotlight, feeling mortified, ashamed, embarrassed, chagrined, and humiliated.

A parent who helps a child recover from a particu-larly humiliating experience will be called blessed. By ignoring the accompanying mistakes, a parent creates an atmosphere that encourages the practice of many activities and the cultivation of new skills.

Dwell on What Is Good and Praiseworthy

Let your children know you are proud of them every time you catch them doing good. Frequent praise and encouragement rewards and reinforces the good. As you praise children you affirm what is good in them. You also build a strong positive relationship between the two of you that allows your child to feel close to you and full of liking for you.

Of course, when you catch a child doing what's not good, you need to explain why. Discourage the bad by punishing immediately. The punishment should be swift, sure, certain, balanced, appropriate, and never abusive. If you have already set a pattern of praise when good is done, that good solid relationship which you have built will not be damaged. React like a lightning strike to the bad when it happens. Then immediately go back to the good so the good is a constant background in your home. Your child will then equate you with feelings of well-being, safety, concern and love—precisely what you want to accomplish.

Some children become defiant in part due to a failed sense of social, athletic, or academic competence. They lash out at parents out of shame, inadequacy, personal weakness, and a lack of feeling autonomous. Your efforts in such cases to help, nurture, and guide are potentially fuel for the fire. You may rub in the child's lack of self-sufficiency and ability to adapt to the daily world.

For example, it is difficult for parents to tutor children with learning disabilities. This is because the fragility of the child's sense of self and self-esteem lead them to rage against parents out of sheer frustration. This in turn enrages parents, who only want to be helpful. In such cases a "disinterested," non-familial tutor is often preferable.

Look to the praiseworthy, the commendable in your prodigal's repertoire of activities. Even if you have to look far into the future to his realizable potential for praise, you can find positive things to dwell on. In so doing you give yourself and your tired-of-it prodigal a refreshing pause from the critical barrage that seems to characterize your relationship.

Keep in mind what your prodigal is capable of becoming. Dwell on that. The self-fulfilling prophecy mechanism could bring about what you dream of, but make sure your dreams fit your prodigal's talents, likes, skills, ambitions, and aptitudes. Be careful not to dream your wants and expectations for him. Never expect him to fulfill your dreams; help him fulfill his. He will fall over himself to get close to you and stay there.

Dwelling on the praiseworthy is contagious. Your prodigal may not catch it overnight. But give whatever time is needed. Don't forget there is still the family bond between you. By shifting to a positive framework of relating, the bond can influence your prodigal, bringing him closer to you and more subject to your influence.

Be your child's most passionate fan club. Even if you have to search diligently for something to be passionate about, find and shout it from the rooftops. Be careful, however, not to use praise as a form of coercion and control. It may be as counterproductive as excessive punishment. Be your child's biggest fan. Lead your child in the right direction through footprints you have already put down so the music of some other pied piper will hold no appeal.

Allow Children to Exercise Their Wings

At the same time, however, give children room to exercise their own wings, under your careful and loving supervision. Children need room to develop their own wings. They need independence and autonomy. And that, after all, is your goal as well as theirs.

Speaking of independence, all children do not assert theirs at the same time in life. Some children show an independent streak early, around age thirteen. Others seem to lag behind, needing nurturing and guidance long after you think they should be leaving the nest and flying alone.

Try releasing your children in factors of 5 percent every birthday from birth to eighteen. At their eighteenth birthday, you may be able to provide the final 15 percent release.

Parents able to give 5 percent release every year will see their children becoming more and more mature as they develop. They will turn more responsible, more independent, never feeling they have to fight for their freedom.

When your children feel ready to fly, they will take the initiative themselves. Anyone who tries to interfere with their flight plans will be vigorously resented.

Releasing your children in increments means staying one step ahead of them. It means giving them freedom quickly, generously, and freely in areas where they have demonstrated competence. In areas where they still need to develop more skill, you need judiciously to reserve your release. If you do see an area of weakness, look for one where you can compensate for what you cannot release. As children tangibly feel the releasing, they will bless you for it. You will find them seeking advice from you in areas where they need help.

Work Yourself Out of a Job

As you continue to release your child into maturity, you will automatically back up with small steps and let development occur without a power struggle. You really don't have much of a choice. Your child's biological development and muscle building are far stronger than you are and will ultimately prevail. You might as well try to command time and tide to stand still.

The job of parenting is to work yourself out of a job. Let it happen. Celebrate its happening. Resist meddling or issuing orders after your child shows the maturity and skill to self-govern and regulate.

Evaluate Your Own Parenting Style

I need to emphasize that if you find yourself the parent of a prodigal, that does not necessarily mean that you had an ineffective parenting style. The prodigal is not automatic proof of your mistakes. There is no direct cause-effect linkage between styles of parenting and parenting outcomes.

Far too many variables impact our children and affect their development and outcome for any great weight to be placed on any one factor. Far too many good parents, who were not permissive or authoritarian, have children who resist every effort to keep them on the right path. Conversely, far too many bad parents find themselves with good children. There is no direct, simplistic explanation.

Having to adjust your parenting style to accommodate the special needs of your prodigal does not mean your parenting style caused the prodigality. But it is worth examining how you are parenting. Doing so need not equal admission of error. Maybe your other children are well-adjusted and happy.

However, at risk of sounding contradictory, parents need to understand that their parenting style is probably the greatest single factor affecting children. Indeed other factors are present and exert their effects. This does not excuse you, however, from the heavy burden of striving always to do the right thing and be the right influence for your children's sake.

CHAPTER 5

Keep Your Own Life on Track Through the Turmoil

THE 1994 NORTHRIDGE EARTHQUAKE shook up a major part of southern California. Victims responded differently depending on inner strengths. We remember seeing newscasts of people digging through the rubble of their homes, trying to find salvageable belongings. We saw them cower in tent homes, afraid to go back to their own houses, or packing cars, trucks, vans with whatever survived the quaking earth and heading to someplace with more stable foundations.

Much of life is like that. We surround ourselves with things, people, events, ceremonies, rituals, and routines that are meaningful to us and our loved ones. When disaster strikes and our carefully arranged configurations suffer damage and displacement, we are shaken. This is neither good nor bad. It simply is. When things are wrenched out of place, some of us hide or run from the carnage without trying to get back to where we were. Others cringe and tremble at the fierce power and terror of the moment, then set about trying to put everything back in its proper place.

When "prodigal child" earthquakes happen, this need not force the rest of your life to a screeching halt. It does not mean all your other roles and responsibilities suddenly cease to exist. Life goes on. Other children need warm and loving parenting. Your partner needs a fully functioning partner to live and love with. Don't let your prodigal turn you into a fire-breathing dragon no one can approach to give or receive love and solace.

You can find nonquaking ground by following a few rules for once more gaining normalcy. Among the rules are these:

1. Don't let yourself get derailed.
2. Establish stable activities.
3. Rely on routine.
4. Focus on intrinsically enjoyable aspects of life.
5. Keep old, reliable friendships alive.

Don't Let Yourself Get Derailed

Keep the common structure of your life steady and intact. Do not allow yourself to become derailed. Derailment can become its own confusing tragedy, adding to your prodigal's predicament. Stable patterns of activities can prop you up externally. Routines operating under their own steam can structure you and wrap structure around you. They can slide you forward, often blessedly mindlessly, through some bad days.

Carol thought her world was coming to an end as she hung up the phone after her conversation with Sergeant Allen. Her son Ken had been arrested again for driving under the influence. He had started sneaking beer at twelve. Teenagers can always find someone willing to get it for them. At seventeen, Ken had lost his license once, had had to go to traffic school, and had been through alcohol treatment. Nothing had worked. His driving was limited to getting to school and to work after classes. Now he had messed up again.

Carol was devastated. She and her husband had done everything they knew how to do. They had spent more money than they could afford trying to salvage their son. At wit's end, Carol finally realized it was she, not her son, who was suffering. So she steadied herself to get back to her life and not allow her son to derail her anymore.

Carol threw herself back into her teaching with a gusto she had not felt since Ken began his downward slide. She realized again teaching was something she loved. She had other children, who sorely missed her when she was emotionally absent because of worry over Ken. She got back into activities and friends she had gradually lost touch with due to Ken's crises.

With her decision not to worry Ken, Carol redesigned her life. She found a rich world full of rewarding things that buoyed her along and structured her into busy activities she had abandoned. Suddenly she had a perspective she had not had for five years. Ken was the one hurting himself. She was out of his loop; he could no longer hurt her too.

Carol didn't stop caring about her son. She did care, but now in healthy and not self-destructive ways. She discovered she had happiness all around her except for Ken. She had friends and activities and family to focus on, good things that were as powerfully real as Ken and his misadventures. These good things had an uplifting life of their own that sustained and refreshed her through the down times when Ken did this or that extraordinarily dumb thing.

Establish Stable Activity Patterns

Activities that have intrinsic value and meaning on their own can continue to have value and meaning on their own. You must rely on such stable activities to inject lightness and soul-refreshing diversion into a heavy and otherwise gloomy phase of existence.

Your life in its totality has meaning far beyond your parenting role. Parenting is just one of many roles you are given to play. As insensitive or uncaring as the statement may seem, your child is not your sole reason for being. Your children will always naturally reside in the core of your being. They are the most important feature of your existence for two decades. Yet they are not, and should not be, the only or even the primary reason for your being on earth.

Your individual existence is substantially more than just parenting children who will soon take flight into their own universes anyway. In the larger scheme of individual lives, childbearing and rearing occupy but a small fraction of the total years given us for living. We are each infinitely more than "reproduction units."

Rely on Routine

Stick to the routines of life that surround you and bear you along. Routines can externally structure life when you are too distressed to think clearly. When the external structure remains in place it can function like an exoskeleton, providing safety, shelter, protection, and support to vulnerable and soft inner workings. Routines can give you a calm-looking external poise that, to your children, looks grounded and collected.

You have set your routines in place for a reason. That reason does not disappear just because one of your children rebels. Indeed, your children need to see you as being stronger than they and the disasters they create, able to brush off disaster like so much dust from collapsing plaster after an earthquake. Sticking to or reestablishing routines makes that obvious to them. Routines also carry us parents along day to day with a continued sense that life has not permanently turned upside-down.

Besides making you look calm externally, routines can calm internally. They give you something to do when you don't know for sure what to do next. Routines can function as calming distractions from what is panicking or distressing you. Moreover, if your next moves pull you back to routine and show that you are still collected, balanced, and centered, your prodigal will be shocked—and possibly dismayed—to see that you're not crumbling. He expects to be reinforced by shocking you. He won't get the chance to experience the diabolical pleasure of saying, "Gotcha!"

When children find out they cannot shake up their parents, several important things happen.

1. Children feel that their parents are in fact strong adults, or at least stronger than they thought (and strength is what they respond to and admire most).

2. Children find more respect for parents who now demonstrate inner strength to move on.

3. They realize parents have a life apart from them. If they derail their own lives it will not derail their parents' lives.

4. Children get a more balanced view of their own importance. They learn they are not the center of the universe.

5. They begin to figure out they are the only ones really getting hurt.

Don't forget that you established routines for a purpose which should not change just because someone at home decides to act up. Stay in touch with the meaning and purpose of routines. Doing so will keep your mind occupied with things other than your prodigal's antics.

Focus on Enjoyable Aspects of Your Life

Studiously focus your attention and thinking on intrinsically enjoyable aspects of your own life—past, present, and future. This will keep you centered on things other than your troubles. It also keeps troubles in perspective so you do not get dragged into feeling useless, helpless, and sorrowful.

Trouble-centered thinking pulls your attention toward what is going wrong. This fills your reflections with disturbing and distressing content. It is not surprising that your mood drops to new lows, life feels not worth living, and you wind up not being good for the rest of your family.

Depression and/or agitation become your new character traits. This makes those close gradually draw away, leaving you alone with your misery. Your new sense of aloneness and estrangement add to your burden of weariness and grief so you sink even lower. Sometimes depression is an underlying trait that precedes and may even foster children's defiance so that they reason, "My parents aren't happy. Why should I accept their values and way of life?"

Remember, before you became a parent you hopefully had a full life. Find comfort in rediscovering some of what made that phase meaningful, productive, and enjoyable. Return to those aspects you previously poured yourself into. What once fascinated and gave you joy can do so again.

Consciously remind yourself of the other aspects of your life. Your parenting self is just a small part of your total self. Develop your non-parenting sides more fully and you will be a better parent not only for your prodigal but your other children as well. The dangerous parent is the one whose life has shrunk to the point where he or she is a parent only. Such an attitude leads to dangerous parent over-involvement. This robs children of developing their own wings of independence.

When you develop your total self you enlarge your identity. You live in dimensions of life that are entirely outside of your prodigal's crises. From those dimensions you find strength to wag your head and wonder how your prodigal does it, how he finds the seemingly limitless ways to get himself into one pickle after another. You might even find yourself chuckling.

When you develop your larger self you draw in elements of identity by which you define yourself. You find within more on which to build a better present and future, more that is accessible to respond to today's crises, and more with which you can describe yourself to yourself. Perhaps, moving to a report card analogy, you can then give yourself a better grade in life. There is more to factor into your total grade point average than just your parenting performance (even assuming your parenting helped foster your child's prodigality, which is questionable).

When you realize there is more to you, your parenting part shrinks to its proper proportion. You have parts to fall back on for comfort and even enjoyment when the going gets tough. Your overall identity is vastly less affected by your admittedly distressing parenting part because there are countless more individual factors in the total equation.

Moreover, you are less likely to forget that you have other children. They are probably doing well in life. And by the way, they probably have a much better perspective on their sibling's troubles than you. The sibling of a prodigal, having no parental investment, can see the prodigal's failures for what they are. Siblings can wag their heads and think, "What a jerk!" Whereas parents sadly, and in deep and dark self-accusatory despair, bury their heads in their hands and think, "What a failure I am!"

It's fair to take at least as much credit for raising an angel or two as it is for you to deal yourself blame for raising a prodigal. In most cases the parent of a prodigal forgets to dwell on the praiseworthiness and achievements of the at-home angel(s).

Deliberately refocusing on the more uplifting parts of your life will pull you into parallel roles, other dimensions of living, that you may have forgotten in the midst of your travails. You realize you do have a life apart from your prodigal, a life worth living, full of people who care. That is where you need to pitch camp. Not "in the valley of the shadow of death," but "in green pastures, beside the still waters."

Keep Old, Reliable Friendships Alive

Keep your life filled with trusted and reliable old friends who can fill your existence with warmth and goodness. They are part of your parallel parts. They can pull you into dimensions of life wholly outside of your troubles. Let them function that way. Let them make you laugh. Let them support you. In the next chapter we will talk more about the importance of friends when you are trying to parent your prodigal.

CHAPTER 6

Share Your Concerns with a Close Friend

OFTEN, THROUGH SHAME, pride, or other reasons, parents keep their family problems private. They do not share family failures even with closest friends and extended family members. Often a prodigal's family is forced to acknowledge trouble because the prodigal's misbehavior is public. Still, however, parents of prodigals tend to keep their fear, pain, and shame to themselves.

For long stretches of time you worry and fear for your child. You lose sleep, appetite, and composure. You become drained of sympathy, empathy, understanding, and compassion because you can give only so long. Then your well of compassion runs dry, leaving only bitterness and resentment bordering on hate. Next you start hating yourself for feeling that way toward your own flesh and blood.

You don't know what to do with your prodigal or your own negative feelings. So you lash out blindly at anyone around you. You splatter your bitterness over those who love you the most and deserve it the least. Your other children, family members, and friends shrink back for self-preservation and protection, leaving you more alone than ever. More injury is added to your agony, for now you are isolated in your private torture.

Sometimes a child's defiance alerts the parents and family system that they are too cut off from external social supports. They come to see that they are an emotionally impoverished family.

Find a Compassionate Confidant

Stop the cycle of torment before it becomes a steep downward spiral that places you in danger of further damaging yourself and those you love. To do so, find someone who can keep your confidence, who knows how to listen and cares in healthy ways. That person could be another family member, a friend, a pastor, a counselor. Your supporter should be someone who will not be swept up in the agonizing drama at your home, who is rock solid, objective, even-tempered, levelheaded.

You don't know anyone like that? Take a mental roll call of family and friends who have shown patience and wisdom. Call your church. See if they have a pastor, deacons, elders, counselors, or others whose strength is compassion and concern. Call your child's school for help.

Take the person you select into your confidence. Talk to him or her as you have never talked to anyone before. Cry and convulse in your confidant's arms. Sob until you cannot shed another tear. Yell, scream, shout, rage. Get it all out of your system so it can do no more harm. Your confidant will know not to take any of it personally because he or she is not involved in what goes on in your home and has no stake in the outcome.

Let your friend be your sounding board, a shoulder to cry on, and once in a while maybe even a punching bag. Let your supporter nourish, nurture, and sustain you for awhile. It's okay to lean on someone when you need to. Knowing your need for support is a mark not of weakness but of wisdom and strength.

Your friend won't shrink from you but will give encouragement when those closest to you distance themselves, perhaps to lick their own wounds.

Sharing Helps You Cope

Sharing your pain with another, talking about it rather than just feeling it, also forces you to articulate what is getting to you. When you do that an interesting thing happens. Instead of registering your feelings emotionally, you register them cognitively and analytically. You move from feelings to analysis of feelings. In doing so you shift gears from the emotional brain center to the problem-solving center.

Technically this is described as moving your processing self from your hypothalamus and limbic system to your cerebral cortex. That major relocation for processing your pain makes all the difference in the world. It takes much of the sting from the emotions that have been paralyzing you.

This is not the same as intellectualizing pain. You are not running or insulating yourself from what pains you. Rather, you are confronting your feeling head-on, directly. You are engaging in a hands-on attack with no holds barred—but with your emotionless, computer-like cerebrum. You make your pain into an object you can analyze. Then you can proceed to carefully dissect what the pain issues.

You can ponder such questions as, What is at stake? What is the investment? Where have I (allegedly) failed? Why am I not able to let go? Why am I killing myself over someone who really doesn't care? Am I over-invested or over-involved in my kid's life? Am I living through my child so his or her failures are mine and make *me* look bad? Am I over-personalizing or identifying with my child's troubles? Am I trying to be the perfect parent to cover over my own felt inadequacies? Does my child's life of woes remind me of my earlier painful, unresolved failures? Am I trying to prove to the world that I'm an okay person because I have perfect kids?

Sharing your pain by articulating it helps. Describing your pain with words makes it an object. Objectifying your pain allows you to step outside and away from it, even if only temporarily, to describe, then analyze, its currents.

Sharing Does Your Body Good

Opening up emotionally to a sensitive listener gets the pain out of your system. Then it can do no further harm, emotionally or physically.

Medicine has for millennia understood the myriad of direct and indirect pathways of connection between emotional and physical well-being. Probably the oldest truth of medicine is that the mind and body are connected in ways that one cannot be affected without affecting the other. Though they differ in the specifics of treatment, systems of medicine the world over converge in understanding that there is a relationship between mind and body. Distress of mind produces distress in body. Agony of soul causes agony of body. This is not breakthrough thinking.

Research by Hans Selye (*The Stress of Life*, 1976) and Holmes and Rahe (*Journal of Psychosomatic Research*, 1967) tells us that the body can take only so much stress (physical, emotional, lifestyle) before it begins to disintegrate, beginning with one's weakest biological system, moving to the next weakest, and so on. When you release the emotion, it more immediately besieges you, yet you still benefit by keeping the net load down to manageable, non-injurious levels.

Adrenalin, cortisol, nonadrenalin—three of the many stress neurotransmitter hormones—can do wonders to ready you for emergency responses. But if they linger in your system too long they tear it down in serious ways. Your body begins to lose its wondrous and remarkable built-in ability to fight off whatever attacks it physically or mentally.

Emotions alert you to things which need your attention. Getting the emotion out is key to moving beyond it. You cannot get beyond what you cannot get out. Yet most sufferers, to their detriment, bravely keep the emotion stoically bottled up when they should be releasing it. True, releasing the emotion does not solve the problem of the prodigal, but it does ease the emotional strain that can turn into physical pain and drain, adding another problem you have to deal with.

Sharing Eliminates Feelings of Isolation and Desolation

Sharing your pain with another also eliminates your feelings of isolation, lonely desolation, and desperation.

Sorrow tends to make us isolate ourselves from others, to rob us of the energy to relate to others. Deliberately and intentionally resisting the self-isolationing "pull away from the world" reaction brings you back into contact with others, back into a relational mode. Sharing brings you back into the interpersonal mechanisms of pain release, putting you in a place where you receive comfort and caring of significant others. They help you carry your load by sometimes carrying it for you.

Sharing Reinforces Intimacy and Vulnerability

Sharing creates and reinforces intimacy and vulnerability. Rather than tensing and hardening in pain, knotting and locking up, cry out and receive comfort.

In receiving comfort you soften and relax. Your soul is soothed. The reactive anger and bitterness that so often harden into the destructive force of self and other-hatred, melts away. Your soul is left renewed, refreshed, soft, and able to heal unscarred. You are strengthened to give of yourself once more.

Share Your Pain with God

There are many promises in Scripture about God's willingness to share with us or bear for us our concerns, worries, and griefs.

Paul told the Philippians, "I can do everything

through him who gives me strength" (4:13). The images of Psalm 23 have been claimed countless times over the millennia by sufferers blessed by the image of a God who accompanies them even through the valley of the shadow of death, so they need fear no evil. The Gospels overflow with stories of Jesus who uses God's power to heal withered hands, blind eyes, tormented souls.

Share your pain with God. Let God hold you, touch you, carry you.

CHAPTER 7

Stay Friends with Your Prodigal

PATIENCE, MERCY, GRACE, and freely given forgiveness are at the heart of effective parenting—whether of a prodigal or an "elder son." These qualities cause you to remain soft and accessible. They must be at the forefront of your being if you go through travails with a difficult child. Without them parents gradually become hard-edged, bitter, spiteful, stinging. They lose all credibility and any ability to attract and draw close to the very person they want most to influence positively.

When relationships become tangled, mangled, and skewed, parents must be the ones to begin realignments. Then as the prodigal sees his parents making efforts to extend and connect, he may well begin reciprocating. Someone has to begin somewhere. You are the adult. You do it.

Cultivate an Atmosphere of Connecting

It is the parents' responsibility to cultivate a home atmosphere of genuine and positive connection. Raising a child in a pleasure-seeking culture is a challenge. Many times you have to say no. But children will trust your no is for their own good if you have a history of enveloping them in a positive relationship and tangibly expressing your care.

Parents seem always to be balancing good and bad experiences. When good outweighs bad, all is well. If, however, the scales tip toward the bad, trouble may be around the corner. Fill the "good" tray to overflowing to compensate for the times when you must do something that feels negative to your child.

I have been a family therapist and psychologist for twenty years. During that time I have never seen a prodigal turn away from genuine and earnest attempts by parents to be caring listeners. Usually the prodigal quickly and voluntarily responds to parents' actions by turning around.

When parents regularly and genuinely ask for sincere feedback on their parenting, children give it, usually respectfully. There are at least two reasons to ask for feedback. First, no matter how perfect parents try to be, no parent is perfect. Children appreciate the chance to say what part of the parenting isn't working for them. Second, when you sincerely seek their input, you give children great respect and standing as real persons in their own right. That is precisely what children strive with all their strength to achieve.

You can help children by walking with them through the dark valleys. Do this by talking to them about their urges, their fascination with violence, injury, pain, destructiveness, hate, meanness. Avoid trying to talk them out of such feelings and fascination, but limit their violent behavior and speech.

Monitor Your Nonverbal Communication

Research indicates that a majority of our communicating is done through nonverbal channels. Such things as facial expressions, hand and body gestures, voice inflection, tone, pitch, rhythm, and tempo of our words reveal the real meaning of our message. Every time we converse with another person we carry on two conversations. One conversation is with words, which we think is primary and most meaningful. The other takes place through nonverbal body language and voice, which convey the "real" message.

As we talk, we surround each word with a host of subtle yet powerful "meaning indicators" that give nuance and inflection to our words and message. Some of the nonverbal messages we send deliberately; others, about 90 percent, we are not aware of. Indeed, if someone were to point out a signal we just sent we would probably deny it or be surprised (or maybe even shocked) by it.

Our nonverbal signals are honest. They tell our listener exactly what we feel. Of course we can consciously bluff, both verbally and nonverbally, but when we communicate spontaneously, our nonverbal language is the more honest. Nonverbal signals bypass the physical hearing of our listeners and register directly on their emotional centers, creating a feeling tone around the verbal message.

Listeners interpret the verbal part of the message in the context of the emotional tone we send out through our nonverbal channels. They respond to the combination. Listeners in turn then respond with a combination of verbal and nonverbal communication.

Being only human, we cannot focus consciously on both levels at once. So we interpret and add meaning without being aware of how it is all happening.

Sometimes, verbal and nonverbal levels of our message contradict each other. Then listeners are puzzled about the real meaning. Bateson describes the clashing of verbal and nonverbal messages as "double bind" statements. Listeners are stopped in their tracks, not knowing how to respond. Eventually they tune out or leave the area of double-bind messages in an attempt to preserve their basic sanity.

For example, when you want to send a loving message to your prodigal, be sure your emotional self truly feels affection toward him. Children and teens seem especially sensitive to nonverbal communication. When your prodigal messes up, you're not required to feel good about the mischief. But you need to feel good about the child despite his mischief. Messages whose verbal and nonverbal components mesh emerge from your ability to combine negative reaction to misbehavior with ongoing love for your child.

Warm, gentle, loving, forgiving gestures reinforce a safe, secure, warm, cuddly, gentle, loving, forgiving connection. Children make mistakes. When parents' nonverbal gestures say "Stay away," while their words say "Come close," the potential prodigal reads the "stay away." When the disliking is great and gripping, the child may adopt opposing and contradictory values to spite his parents. This sets the stage for pain and suffering on both sides.

Analyze the Blame

Throughout this book we are trying to walk a fine line between releasing parents from blame for prodigals and asking them to confront their possible contributions to the development of prodigality. There is no easy way to do this. We can only suggest that you wrestle deeply with the tension and explore the possibility that you are missing something.whenever you too easily excuse or blame yourself.

Here we want to focus on the fact that one important part of parenting the prodigal involves and indeed begins with deep, honest, soul-searching to minimize your own contributions to the problem. Instead of starting by blaming the prodigal, wanting him to shape up first and fast, parents need to analyze the situation. They need to take their share of the blame (though only their share, as we have been stressing).

I cannot tell you how many parents have dumped their prodigals at my office door with the comment, "Fix 'im quick. I can't stand 'im." These parents are incredibly resistant to the idea that their child's prodigality may involve a two- or three-person dance.

When dealing with our prodigal's misbehavior, our first tendency is to read and interpret his actions negatively. From then on we look for collisions of will. Our negative reaction guarantees that more collisions will occur. This is not because they were going to anyway but because we have already attached blame to the prodigal. We need to stop and analyze. Are we blaming the prodigal because of his misdeeds? Or are we trying to cover up what we are responsible for?

Our human tendency is to rid ourselves of blame

for errors or mistakes. Thus we automatically and unconsciously wash ourselves clean of whatever we may have done badly. This makes us vulnerable to blaming only our children, not ourselves, for their prodigality. This is when things go wrong between you and your prodigal, pushing him further away from you.

Then guess what. Your prodigal blames you. There you both stand, arms akimbo, staring daggers at each other, blaming each other for the badness, neither willing to back down one inch.

This blame cycle can continue indefinitely if neither side takes the initiative to see the situation from the other's perspective. Such a stand-off can go on for years or decades, each of you erecting fences where, except for a deep initial misunderstanding, there could have been closeness, harmony, and affection. Over time, misinterpretations pile onto misunderstandings until the multiple layers seem too painful and deep to cut through. Feeling and believing their alienation has become too complicated to sort out, the combatants give up on ever connecting. They walk away from a relationship that is truly salvageable.

If it is caught early, this scenario is correctable. Two things must be done. First, look at things from the other person's angle. Second, acknowledge your imperfection as a parent and take responsibility for making a midcourse correction that could end the standoff. As the adult you must take the lead. Your prodigal will probably respond by meeting you step for step, more than likely dissolving the impasse, leaving both of you marching in the same direction.

When children see that their parents are willing to

admit their mistakes, take responsibility for them, and make mid-course corrections, it wows them. They suddenly see that their parents are not high and mighty royals, holier than thou, sickeningly self-righteous strangers. Rather, their parents are real people, honest and approachable, mortals, trying to do an enormously complicated job well. They make mistakes but learn from, acknowledge, and correct them. They sincerely want to be connected to their children.

Parents can still be parents in user-friendly ways. Authority can be established in comfortable ways. Find them and use them. Wear your authority in good humor, surround your instructions with solid explanations, be warm and loving, and get on with it. Expect your child to obey. If he does not, fashion some appropriate consequence that fits the crime and teaches a lesson. Deliver it calmly so the child connects the punishment with his crime, not with your anger.

As you fly through life it may be difficult to keep in touch with your own gauges. Slow down long enough to do it anyway. True, there are built-in difficulties to work around. It is hard to do things and watch yourself do them; your mind focuses on doing or watching, never both simultaneously. But it can be done. Keep a careful eye on how you are doing as seen through the eyes of your child. If you can keep that perspective, you will self-correct before difficulties begin. If you do not correct course, you will see—perhaps from the corner of your eye—that problems are coming. Bridge the rift early before the break is too large to deal with.

CHAPTER 8

Realize That Your Prodigal Will Grow Up

SOONER OR LATER—sometimes a lot later than parents hope for—difficult youths grow up. Their tomfoolery yields to the arrival of weight-bearing adulthood and full acceptance of the responsibilities adults carry.

Maturation is a process that rolls slowly, steadily, cumulatively, and unstoppably forward. But some children, by their biological nature, are late bloomers. There's not a thing anyone can do to change that. Nor should you try. As long as the clock's hands continue to move forward, at whatever speed, leave the clock alone and don't bemoan its pace. The clock is moving at just the right speed for its host.

Some children grow up so fast their parents wonder what happened. Late bloomers, however, need the gifts of time and patience as their immutable genetic clocks bring them into adulthood. Sooner or later all males finally have to shave. Some shave daily at thirteen, others sport peach fuzz until they are twenty. However, by mid-twenties, except for the hormonal anomaly, most males are shaving or bearded.

The brain, with all its complex centers and functions, continues to develop until late teens. And for many, full adulthood does not arrive until late twenties —or sometimes even later. Nothing you or your child can do will hurry it up. No amount of wishing, pushing, praying, tinkering, bribing, or doctoring will change a thing. To try to hurry it up will only create bigger problems. If you leave it alone and let it do its own work, simple biological maturation, controlled by the pituitary gland, will complete its mission.

A great deal of harm can result from trying to speed things ahead of your child's readiness. Children's behavior reflects the state of their biological development and biologically driven psychological development. Human biology and developmental psychology are inextricably intertwined; biological development drives psychological development.

Your job as parent is to create a safe climate for this development to occur at whatever speed it occurs. You are supposed to be the nurturer, the nourisher of that person in the making, not its driving engineer.

Children Come in Infinite Varieties

Children are not cookie-cutter commodities. They are not shapeless lumps of sculpting clay to be molded into whatever shape parents want. Children have their own genetically written temperaments that include natural skills, inborn talents, innate aptitudes, good-ats, not-good-ats, natural affinities, almost unchangeable natural likes and dislikes. We might envision children as falling into several broad types.

Explorers "boldly go where no one has gone before." They drive their parents nuts in the process. Explorers aren't bad; they're just unique. They march to a different drummer, one their parents cannot hear, fathom, or even imagine. They are creators of culture, not its sheep.

Be patient and understanding. Work with and not against explorers. Don't push them into a mold that does not fit. Who knows, that explorer may become the next Edmund Hillary, who in 1953 was the first to reach the summit of Mt. Everest and return.

By some internal, irrepressible imperative, *mavericks* do things their own way. They work independently. Do not interfere with their plan. They have their own way of learning. Respect such ways; don't meddle.

Be patient and understanding. Work with and not against mavericks. Who knows, that maverick may become the next Thomas Edison. Or Albert Einstein, who allegedly said not a word until age five then started talking in whole sentences. When asked why he was so long silent, Einstein simply said he had been thinking.

Mischief-makers look for ways to introduce interesting twists and surprises. They aim to inject the unexpected and funny into otherwise routine and boring ways of doing things.

Be patient. Laugh with them, work with and not against them. Who knows, the mischief-maker may become the next Kurt Lewin, the famous sociologist whose breakthrough research methods (the hidden camera) and clever research assistant (Allen Funt) gave birth to "Candid Camera."

Strong-willed children persist in the face of monumental opposition. They will, with maddening perseverance, find a way to work something out.

Be patient and understanding. Work with and not against them. The stubborn child may surprise you and become the next J. Robert Oppenheimer. Along with Einstein and other scientists, mathematicians, and engineers, Oppenheimer found the way to make the atomic bomb. He then became its vocal critic, losing everything he had dreamed of by opposing its use on humanitarian grounds.

Dreamers are loners, out to lunch, out of it, out of synch with everything and everybody. They walk around in a daze, rarely talking to anyone. Dreamers walk into walls because their minds are in a different time zone or perhaps even universe.

Be patient and understanding. Work with and not against dreamers. They may dream up whole new ways of conceptualizing the space/time continuum. Who knows, that dreamer may become the next Peter Hawking, a theoretical physicist and mathematician said to be Einstein's equal in the late twentieth century.

Pioneers are independent and self-directing. They go against the grain of public opinion. They wind up rubbing almost everyone the wrong way because they initiate fresh and sometimes brash ways of seeing and approaching things.

Be patient and understanding. Work with and not against pioneers. Who knows, that pioneer may become the next Dr. Simmelweiss, the unpopular but brilliant physician who developed the antiseptic technique in medicine. He infuriated the entire medical world by having the temerity to suggest that doctors themselves, by not washing their hands and sterilizing their equipment, could be responsible for spreading death and disease.

The list of positive examples of out-of-the-norm, and perhaps frustrating and maddening types is endless. Each of the preceding types has a negative as well as positive potential. Each example could have had a different ending had the child been parented incorrectly.

When you reinforce that which is positive and patiently bear with the sometimes negative, the outcome will be good. Your child may not make the history books but will end up a wonderful, unique, satisfying person. The critical variable is to see and work with the good. Play the hand you have been dealt and you will be pleased, if not thrilled, with the outcome.

Children Are Their Own Persons

What genes have written no one can alter. Whatever your thwarted ambitions may have been, put them firmly aside with respect to raising your child. Children are their own persons and must discover and pursue the talents and aptitudes nature has given them. To do otherwise is a tragedy.

Carl was on a trajectory that left his parents cold. Whatever they said, Carl said the opposite. Whatever they told Carl to do, he did the opposite. His parents tried everything. Nothing worked. All he ever wanted to do was sit in his room and scribble on pads of paper. School was not high on his list of priorities. He began to cut classes, then entire days.

Finally, to avoid the pressure, he just left home. He

quit washing his clothes and replaced them with whatever was cheapest in the thrift shops. He let his hair grow longer than any other child's, stopped shaving, didn't comb his hair or beard. He adopted the ways of a vagabond. He crashed wherever he could, and sometimes did not bother to eat at all. His friends were misfits and dropouts like him.

All the while his parents tried their best to remain open and continue to love him. But it became too much for them. In self-defense they wrote him off.

One day, sitting in a barber shop waiting for his favorite barber to cut his hair, Carl's dad thumbed through a recent copy of an alternative magazine that happened to be lying on the stack. He wanted to see how the "weirdos and hippies" lived. Stunned, he saw his son's name as a contributing poet.

He read what his son had submitted and saw for the first time that he was a talented writer. Coming from a long line of investment bankers, Carl had broken the mold and became a poet. The boy didn't know derivatives from dividends, but he knew iambic pentameter. Rhythm and meter sang to him like profit and loss statements sang to his dad. Carl had the same intuitive feel for verse that his dad had for putting together a business plan and seeking venture capital. Both sought quality—just in different worlds.

That night Carl got a call from a friend of a friend who said his dad was looking for him. A nervous phone call led to a tearful reconciliation between father and son, who had not seen each other in years. That call began a journey that led father and son back together and began a new relationship in which Carl's dad underwrote his son's education, not at Wharton but at Berkeley. Much of the son's poetry still has to do with the pain of estrangement and the thrill of reunion.

Children will bless parents who are instrumental in helping him them find their niche and encourage them in it. Deciding what children should be, then proceeding to push and shove them toward it will probably cause them to resist you all the way. Soon resistance turns into a never-ending struggle between parent and child, with no one winning and both hating the other because of it.

On the other hand, and just as tragic, children may fear parents' displeasure, so they go along with parents' plans until they are on their own. Then they abandon the parents' plans and all has been wasted. Both the parents' efforts and precious time are lost for such children. This is time they could have used to learn, develop, and perfect natural skills and abilities. They may never make up the lost time and may resent parental meddling in and derailing of their choices.

What You Need to Give

None of this means that you indulge your child's whims and fancies. You don't. But you do carefully observe your children's natural rhythms and interact with them accordingly.

There is always a place for moral discipline and ethical teaching, teaching that is universally applicable and relevant to all types and styles of temperament. There are common disciplines of heart, soul, and mind, and lessons in practical living everyone should take in to become a valued member of community life.

Parents cannot become lax in such instruction. When it comes to the practical path your children should walk, though, let their talents direct their steps. Let their natural aptitudes establish their pathway. Let them walk their God-given walk.

Work with your child's natural aptitudes and abilities, not against them. Carefully place yourself in your child's world and perspective from day one. Enter your child's world as ally, not adversary or enemy.

When you do this your child will treasure you and admire what you have done. Your child will then automatically hold you up as someone worth getting and staying close to and will never leave your side until biological and psychological maturation leads to a separate existence. Even then, your child will treat your example as a treasure map to be carefully followed. Your influence and teaching can last forever.

CHAPTER 9

Forgive Endlessly

IF YOU DO NOT LEARN to forgive your prodigal, all the hard times you have both been through will have served little purpose.

We cannot emphasize enough the importance of forgiveness in the reconciliation process. As we explored earlier, forgiving does not mean that you must feel good about the prodigal's mischief before you send a positive message. It means feeling good about the child despite mischief. You can hate acting out without hating the child. Forgiving allows you to wipe clean all slates. Your prodigal will feel and eventually thank you for the cleansing effect of a fresh start.

The kind of forgiveness you need to offer is unlimited, unreserved, unconditional—and unearned.

Why Forgiving Is Critical

Hurt, anger, bad memories, grudges, and resentments pile up. If you don't repeatedly clean the slate you will relate to your prodigal through these built-up negative emotions. Accumulated pain and resentments will sour interactions with your child, making a bitter enemy of him. Remember the power of self-fulfilling prophecy.

Forgiving your prodigal achieves two purposes. It gives the prodigal a fresh start. And it cleans the slate for you, so you can perceive the prodigal as though he had never offended you, your family, and (in your eyes) the whole world.

Your prodigal will consistently push the meaning of "screw-up" to new dimensions. This means you will have to push the meaning of forgiveness to new dimensions. Your prodigal will not deserve nor earn forgiveness. But he will desperately need it to stand before you, the world, and himself with "face," without the stains of prior transgressions.

The renewal that comes from forgiveness benefits the cleansed one and the cleanser. It frees the prodigal from spending the rest of his life trying to undo the harm he did earlier. And it frees you from dragging along the burden of ugly baggage that only impedes progress and hurts you.

Forgiving Is Not Denying Your Feelings

Forgiving does not mean denying feelings of grief or deep bitterness. Forgiving does not mean driving them inward so they later appear in physical or emotional symptoms. Feelings of inexpressible rage, unfathomable grief, overwhelming confusion, indescribable worry, or a sudden and terrifying urge to strangle are normal.

Do not deny these emotions if they are part of your reaction. Obviously you do not have to act on feelings. But feelings are real and need to be gotten out of your system in some constructive way. Acknowledging and then sharing them is critical.

That is why it is important to stay close to a carefully selected, trusted, understanding, calm, mature friend. Your supporter should be a person who can, in confidence, be your crying shoulder when crying is appropriate, or a punching bag when you need verbally to discharge smoldering anger.

The brave soul who keeps it all in so the world thinks she or he is coping is fair game for an ulcer, a heart attack, a stroke. Even if you escape the physical results you may become a monster to live with. Don't add separation or divorce to your woes. Bottled-up anger damages your physical and emotional health and affects everything you do. Anger will affect your ability to parent others in the family who still need parenting and to love a partner who needs you as much as you need him or her.

Forgiving Is Not Making Excuses

Minimizing misbehavior—yours in parenting or your prodigal's in rebelliousness—does nothing to remedy or understand the situation. Don't allow yourself to turn from what is not pretty. Don't paper over unhealthy family patterns by simplifying the situation or making sentimental reconciliation efforts.

What you want to accomplish is healing between you and your prodigal. This requires action by both. Correction and healing come only from grasping the scope and sources of problems. This may mean that you have to acknowledge your contribution to problems. After facing whatever led to the troubles, you can deliberately and conscientiously correct your part in them, even if that means exposing your errors.

No one likes to face personal blemishes. But healing requires both parent and prodigal to face their flaws. Excusing or minimizing parental negligence or prodigal waywardness remedies nothing.

Forgiving Is Not Rescuing

Forgiving prodigals does not mean rescuing them every time they mess up. Children should be helped once or twice when they inadvertently or carelessly get into trouble. Some children learn fast and well; one flop will do it. Some need two lessons for important learning to sink in.

If your prodigal deliberately continues to step out of line and you continue to rescue him, you will create and reinforce the idea that your role is to rescue, not teach. If he gets in a jam, let him pull himself out. Unless the consequences of his behavior are life-threatening, the best teaching is to step aside.

Parents must do for their children what they cannot do for themselves due to weakness or lack of skill. But to do everything for them teaches them to be lazy and irresponsible. Self-rescuing teaches resourcefulness. It also helps prodigals develop respect for consequences and forces them to think several laps ahead of their actions. Self-rescuing develops the strength and know-how prodigals will need to pull out of subsequent messes. Self-rescuing helps create the internal resource and habits of self-reliance and independence.

People don't develop strength by having others lift loads for them. They don't develop self-reliance or independence by traveling a road someone else laid out for them and with fuel someone else paid for.

What Is Forgiveness?

Now that we have explored what forgiveness is not, what *is* it? In *Caring Enough to Forgive/Caring Enough to Not Forgive* (Regal Books, 1981, p. 31) David Augsburger says that "forgiveness is a journey of many steps . . . taken carefully, thoughtfully, and with deep reflection."

Augsburger lists the steps as—

1. to see the other as having worth again, regardless of wrongdoing;

2. to see the other as equally precious again, in spite of the pain felt;

3. to cancel demands on the past, recognizing that changing the unchangeable is impossible;

4. to work through the anger and pain felt by both in reciprocal trusting and risking until genuineness in intention is perceived and repentance is seen by both to be authentic;

5. to drop the demands for an ironclad guarantee of future behavior and open the future to choice, to spontaneity, to the freedom to fall again;

6. to touch each other deeply, to feel moved in warmth, love, compassion, to celebrate it in mutual recognition that right relationships have been achieved.

Forgiveness is an ongoing act, a process with several phases. The first phase is for forgivers to make a conscious effort to set aside a need for revenge.

Next forgivers must consciously cancel out demerits and no longer hold them against prodigals.

Third, forgivers deliberately and with effort reorient themselves toward prodigals so they are no longer at a distance.

Notice that so far your feelings have not figured into your actions. You are not waiting for the spirit to move you or for your prodigal to make the first move. Actually, your primary feelings so far are those which make you want to strangle your prodigal. *Will* the necessary adjustments; positive feelings will follow later.

The fourth phase involves consciously and deliberately directing gestures of warmth and closeness toward your prodigal. You invite the transgressor back into relationship with you. Your feelings are still not the guiding force.

The fifth phase occurs when the prodigal makes tentative and nervous moves back toward relationship with you. You respond with further gestures of deepening invitation and warmth.

Feelings of true closeness begin to emerge in the sixth phase. They are tiny filaments of attachment at first. Then as the prodigal comes closer, the filaments thicken into cords.

In the final phase of forgiveness true emotional forgiveness occurs. Pain fades and joy replaces the urge to kill.

Unfortunately, most parents either stand still or remove themselves from the prodigal while waiting for the spirit to move them. Yet the spirit often does not begin moving until very late in the forgiving process. This is why it is helpful to think of forgiveness as a multiphase sequence of actions directed by one's will and willingness to forgive.

If you refuse to forgive, you will find yourself written out of your prodigal's life due not to his but your hardness. If you have not had a forgiving heart, when he does turn around you will be history. And you will stay history until you find and extend forgiveness generously and without strings.

How You Know When You Have Truly Forgiven

The model prayer taught by Jesus says, "Forgive us our debts as we forgive our debtors." The Greek word translated "forgive" in this verse is *aphiemi*, which means to send away. It is the same word used in Luke 4:39 when Jesus rebuked the fever in Peter's mother-in-law. Jesus "bent over her and rebuked the fever, and it left [aphiemi] her. She got up at once and began to wait on them."

That is the kind of forgiveness David speaks of when he says God has removed our transgressions from his mind "as far as the east is from the west" (Ps. 103:12). It is the forgiveness Jeremiah invokes in saying that God promised to "forgive their wickedness and will remember their sins no more" (Jer. 31:34). It is the kind of reaction the father of the prodigal kept alive in his heart until his son returned home.

CHAPTER 10

Make Your Home a Welcoming Shelter

EVERYONE HAS A SELF-REGULATING, self-organizing, built-in, and dynamic center. This center points them toward that place their heart calls home.

Ideally home is a place of return, safe shelter, protection, warmth, renewal, quietness. Ideally home is a place of laughter, pleasure, contentment, fulfillment.

There will be times, of course, when craziness, chaos, and tension invade your home. To the best of your ability and the limits of your endurance, however, make your home the kind of place where everyone experiences warmth and love.

Make your home that warm place that pulls. Children bolt when forces at home push away rather than pull toward. When the pain of staying is greater than the gain, when the gain is no longer worth the cost, then the child tries to escape. Human nature abhors disharmony and strives to banish clashing elements and forces. When parents safeguard their children while creating a warm hearth, children will think twice about leaving.

There are, of course, painful exceptions. Some children are so bent on hell-raising that nothing can constrain them. These kids are so sure they know it all that parents can only step aside. They can only let their prodigals crash into the nearest wall and hope to heaven that the crash does not kill.

After they crash, it is hoped parents are prepared to pick up the pieces and tenderly carry them home without being judgmental or rubbing their prodigal's nose in their messes. This is where this path diverges from "tough-love" which would advise letting children pick up their own pieces.

Slamming the door and bolting it will teach a lesson—but not about love. It will teach the prodigal that he cannot ever return. It will teach about self-righteousness, unforgiveness, hardness, noncompromise, revenge, condemnation. What the prodigal needs are forgiveness, softness, warmth, flexibility, healing, acceptance, love, mercy, understanding, grace, reconciliation—all those qualities associated with "home."

Protect the Peace and Harmony

When clashing elements and forces disrupt harmony, human nature seeks to jettison the discordant factors. Clearly, you cannot jettison a child. But there are things you can do to keep your home a shelter and let your prodigal realize you intend to keep it that way.

First, no matter what your child says or does, *stay calm*. Whatever else may be going on inside you should stay inside. Your prodigal wants you to be hysterical; that's his payoff. Don't give it. This refusal gives your prodigal the sense that you are basically grounded, unshaken, in control. If you lose your cool you may exchange words that will wound your relationship. If you feel as if you are about to explode, take a break. Get away from the scene and collect yourself. Do some deep breathing, listen to relaxing music, go for a walk or run. Let your surging adrenaline return to rest levels.

The aim is to model *self*-control, not to control or dominate the interaction with your child to bolster your ego. The important thing is for your prodigal to see that you are in control of your reaction to his antics, even if you are going ballistic inside.

Second, *every child has a lever*. Whatever lever you use should never be physically or emotionally abusive. Neither should it be unkind, mean-tempered, harshly worded, or angrily delivered. Announce your intention ahead of time with good-natured playfulness. The goal is to concoct something that will benignly embarrass the prodigal. This takes a bit of boldness and hamming it up on your part. Then be sure to do it if necessary. Don't threaten without follow-through. The teen will probably break into raucous laughter and exclaim, "You're kidding! You wouldn't dare do that!"

One of the most common and powerful of levers is social embarrassment. One parent I know warned his child what he would do if his son ever created a disturbance during a church service. When it happened, the father got up from a pew in the back of the sanctuary and paraded down the center aisle to the front where the young people usually sat. He squeezed wordlessly himself in next to his son and held his hand for the remainder of the service. He warned his son; he followed through.

Another father announced to his son that, if he got any more calls from the attendance office about cutting classes, he would take two weeks off work. He would go to school with his son. He would dress like him, hang around with his friends, talk like him, walk like him, slouch around like him, comb his hair like him, attend all his classes, flirt with the girls his son thought were "babes." After all, he reasoned to his son, "if the life you're living is so good, there must be something to it. Why not try it. Hey, we could even be pals and live it together."

Of course his son didn't think his straitlaced father would follow through. He shrugged off what he considered just one more empty threat. But the morning after yet another call came from the attendance office. To his horror, the son saw his dad come to breakfast dressed in grunge style carefully put together with pickings from the local thrift store. The son begged the father not to go to school, and to the son's infinite relief the father didn't, and there have been no more missed classes.

One mother told her daughter that from now on she would drive her to school since the daughter seemed to have trouble getting there on time on her own. On the morning the personal chauffeuring was to begin, the mother slid behind the wheel in curlers, facial mask, and a threadbare bathrobe (with pink floppy slippers). The daughter went nuts, but the mother calmly proceeded.

When they arrived at school, the mother made it a point to drop off her daughter at the busiest corner of the campus, where all her daughter's friends hung out.

The mother got out, opened her daughter's door, and started toward the attendance office, leaving the car idling in the intersection. Traffic stopped. Everyone gawked. The daughter wanted to drop through the sidewalk. She instantly agreed there would be no more lateness problems. And there haven't been.

Third, *you still make the rules*. In fact, you may have to make two different sets of rules, one for the cooperative kids, another for the prodigal. Parenting the prodigal calls for you to react differently than toward a child who welcomes openness, honesty, authenticity. Parents who desperately want their children's approval tend to tolerate unacceptable behavior. But your prodigal needs to hear, "I will no longer passively accept violent language or behavior toward me." Don't be afraid to use alternative rules even when the prodigal whines that you "don't make Jennifer do that!"

Simply explain to your complaining prodigal that you will treat him like his brothers and sisters when he cooperates and behaves. Explain that different behaviors call for different remedies and strategies.

Fourth, in dealing with a prodigal you need to *learn non-confrontive interference*. Think of it as surrounding your prodigal with your presence night and day. You will not literally have to tail your child everywhere he goes, but you need to convince him that you'll do so if that's what it takes. Interfering non-confrontively is not bullying or threatening; it is simply being present all the time.

Keep the Door Open and the Porch Light Lit

Your job is intentionally, actively, and deliberately to create a home atmosphere that is warm, caring, supportive, forgiving. You may not bat a perfect thousand, but if you connect more often than you miss, your family will find treasure in your home.

People gravitate toward those whose arms are extended in welcome and understanding. Knowing that the door is always open, the porch light is on, and the welcome mat is out will draw your child home like a magnet. No matter how hard it is, or how much bad blood has flowed between you and your child, keep the door open and the light on.

It is easy to shut the door and figure that your prodigal has earned his or her just rewards. Technically, that may be a valid point. But are you trying to prove a point or prevent a shipwreck? Shutting your child out may help you deal with your vexation, but it does nothing to help the prodigal recover his or her balance and regain the right path. However strong the temptation, keep the homing beacon lit so your prodigal can find his or her way toward safe harbor.

When times get especially bad, the thought of a porch light and an open door may be the only direction-finding device your prodigal has. The vision may save your child time and again, though you may never know how it helped. Turning off the light and slamming the door may destroy the last hope for the prodigal, leaving him or her in darkness without bearings and without hope. The welcome mat at the open door may remind him of what can yet be if your child just heads in that direction.

This is the kind of home the prodigal remembered when he or she was out in the fields feeding pigs. "When he came to his senses, he said . . .'I will set out and go back to my father and say to him: Father, I have sinned against heaven and against you. I am no longer worthy to be called your son; make me like one of your hired men.' So he got up and went to his father." He remembered the safe shelter of home.

Never Give Up Hope!

Derrick was beyond control. At age fourteen he split from home to run with the big guys. His parents, scared to death that something bad had or might happen to him, reported him a runaway. When found he was made a ward of the court. Derrick was placed in a foster home from which he also split. He was attracted to the exciting life he had seen his older friends live but could not yet create for himself. Sometimes he went to school, but only for its social life and the easy availability of girls and drugs.

Derrick looked older than his age and was good looking. He was cool, slick, had a way with words and could glide through ticklish situations with finesse he had seen in older mentors. He soon exhausted his friends' offerings of hospitality and lived on the streets by the strength of his wits.

His parents kept reaching out to him, letting him know he was always welcome back home. His old room was as it had always been. His parents had never emotionally moved him out to erase their pain by removing all traces of him.

Finally Derrick ran out of gas. He was picked up for

vagrancy. Because he was still a minor his parents were called. They immediately came to claim their street-smudged son and treated him like the father did in the parable of the prodigal.

Not all stories end like Derrick's. Parents of prodigals are sometimes called by coroners who need a positive ID. Fortunately parents are far more often called by police needing a home to send a child to. Except when death ends the story, there is always hope.

Never give up hope that your prodigal will come home. The kind of hope you need is that which drives a committed caregiver to hang in there in the face of no evidence that anything is working—at least not yet. This kind of hope is the muscle behind the extending of one kindness after another despite the absence of gratitude or effects—at least for now. This hope is the wind that keeps you moving forward, looking for better days ahead in the face of nothing but bad. This hope drives and sustains and can be at the core of a positive-outcome, self-fulfilling prophecy.

This hope is put directly into effect by you; you control it. You can turn it on and you can turn it off, thus affecting to some degree the direction, destination, and destiny of your prodigal. Just because your prodigal takes off in the opposite direction from the one you would have your child travel does not mean your prodigal is out of your field of influence.

Hope keeps you centered and focused on better things, which you trust are just over the horizon, unseen but expected. It keeps you centered on the positive and uplifting. Human psychological functioning is such that people always—always—focus on the more disturbing elements in the scenes before them. Our eyes always land on what is not right or disturbs us about the picture.

A parent confronted by an upsetting prodigal tends to obsess over the problem until both of you are sick to death of your nagging. Then your child will tell you with undisguised bitterness precisely where you can take your nagging. Your prodigal will be off on his or her merry way, leaving you without resolution and more shaken.

Often the adolescent rebel is still as controlled by his or her parents as before the child's rebellion. The prodigal just reverses the vectors (a vector is a direction—of travel, action, force, or thinking) his or her parents chose for the prodigal. The rebel is like the stubborn two-year-old who has just learned to say no for the very first time. The parents are in control, they just need to control differently. The same thing occurs again at puberty. The prodigal who reverses vectors is said to be operating "counter-dependently," not independently. Even though it feels to the prodigal like independence, it is not.

As long as you see your prodigal making reverse vector choices, rest assured you still have a great deal of influence over your child. Don't let your child know that you know, just rest assured that it's true and calmly keep faith that all is not lost. Also remember that once your prodigal starts making reverse-vector choices, you must move to parenting by quiet, consistent example, not by crack-the-whip orders. If you don't make that critical shift, all will be lost.

Have a Feast and Celebrate the Homecoming

Every parent can relate to the prodigal's father as he waited for his son to come home. What parents have not stayed awake until long after midnight waiting for the sound of a car door that let them know their child was home? How many of us have waited day after day for the phone to ring, and for a tentative voice to say, "Hi, Mom. It's me." Others have searched the faces on crowded city streets, hoping to spot their prodigal sons or daughters.

Our story tells us that the father saw his son "while he was still a long way off." He had searched the horizon every day his son was gone for that pathetic figure. When he saw the filthy and haggard prodigal from "far off" he jumped for joy. He was "filled with compassion" and "ran to his son, threw his arms around him and kissed him." He knew it was time for a celebration. "For this son of mine was dead and is alive again; he was lost and is found."

The father knew how to respond correctly to his prodigal's return and did it perfectly, rejoicing upon reunion. Open arms, open heart, open joy should greet the prodigal. Experience has taught the prodigal the hard way. The prodigal does not need his or her nose rubbed in his or her mistakes. It's humbling enough to limp home. Don't add to your child's shame.

A dear friend of mine remembers the day her daughter left an oppressive, crushing religious commune that had forced her to deny her family, her church, and all her former friends. Every family member, except one sister and her mother, had given up on her because of her open contempt for them. She was in deadly fear of what the cult "family" would do to her if she did not conform.

When she finally appeared at her mother's door and asked if she could move back home, the mother was overwhelmed with joy. The mother remained concerned, however, not to do or say something to send her daughter back into the overprotective arms of the commune. So she provided a welcome that was sensitive and quiet yet joyful and sincere. The mother provided the right welcome. The daughter would not have enjoyed a public celebration. Too much healing still needed to be done to detach from the strong bonds of the cult.

However you do it, when your prodigal comes home, "have a ball." "Bring the fatted calf and kill it . . . have a feast and celebrate." Or just show how happy you are to have your beloved child back home, safe and secure, with hugs, kisses, tears, and a lot of forgiveness. It's time to briefly spoil her or him. Growing up or growing tired has taken place. Reconciliation is beginning to happen. Welcome it, rejoice in it, nurture it.

At this time your prodigal is most easily influenced and moldable. Show love, reunion, and unfailing caring by example. Demonstrate what "family" really means. Once home the prodigal has a new chance to heal and absorb healthy values. Cloak those values in love and care, and your prodigal will absorb them as a dry sponge absorbs moisture.

Sometimes parents do all they know to entice their children home but still wind up with permanently alienated prodigals. Some children, for whatever reasons, can learn only the hard way. The parents of such children should not blame but comfort.

They should keep the door open, the porch light lit, the prodigal's bed turned down, and the pillow fluffed with a chocolate mint lovingly placed upon it.

The Author

DR.S. RUTHERFORD MCDILL JR. is a forensic/clinical psychologist. He is the father of three grown children, Erin, Darren, Lindsay, in whom he is well pleased.

McDill received a B.A. in zoology from the University of California (1969), and M.A. in psychology from Pepperdine University (1973), and a Ph.D. in clinical psychology from USIU San Diego (1981).

Employed by the California Corrections Department, he has been active in building treatment programs in the prison setting, for churches and other organizations. He is semiretired, which means he works only fifty hours a week these days.

He had been in practice since 1974. In addition to activities related to clinical and forensic practice, he has organized seven church-based counseling centers as well as a free-standing nonprofit training center for therapists. He has written *Shattered and Broken: Domestic Violence in the Christian Community* (Revell, 1991), *Raising Safety Smart Kids* (Thomas Nelson, 1993), and seems always to have a book in process.

McDill has appeared on television and radio programs to discuss issues touching on social psychology and the individual. He teaches on the graduate and undergraduate levels.

When not working, McDill and his wife, Lynn, enjoy relaxed country living in the mile-high oak and pine covered mountains and valleys where they have made their home. "Brik," as his friends know him, and Lynn attend Good Shepherd Lutheran Church in the small town of Tehachapi, California.